Beginner's Guide to
Revelation

Beginner's Guide to
Revelation

A Jungian Interpretation

Robin Robertson

NICOLAS-HAYS
York Beach, Maine

First published in 1994 by
Nicolas-Hays, Inc.
P. O. Box 612
York Beach, ME 03910-0612

Distributed to the trade by
Samuel Weiser, Inc.
P. O. Box 612
York Beach, ME 03910-0612

Library of Congress Cataloging-in-Publication Data
Robertson, Robin
    Beginner's guide to Revelation : a Jungian interpretation / by
Robin Robertson.
        p.   cm.
    Rev ed. of: After the end of time. c1990.
    Includes bibliographical references and index.
    1. Bible. N.T. Revelation--Miscellanea.   I. Robertson, Robin.
        After the end of time.   II. Title.
    BS2825.5.R63   1994
    228'.06--dc20   94-18306
    ISBN 0–89254–030–3   CIP
BJ

Cover art is a painting titled "The Search Party."
Copyright © 1994 Rob Schouten.

Printed in the United States of America

99 98 97 96 95 94
10 9 8 7 6 5 4 3 2 1

Typeset in 11 point Palatino

The paper used in this publication meets the minimun requirements of
the American National Standard for Permanence of Paper for Printed
Library Materials Z39.48–1984.

To my parents, whose love and support of an unusual and difficult child gave me the courage to follow my own path in life. That path has led ineluctably to this book.

And to my friend, Mike Uranga, for whom this material had special significance.

CONTENTS

LIST OF ILLUSTRATIONS

ACKNOWLEDGMENTS

I thank *Psychological Perspectives* for permission to adapt articles published in 1987, 1988, and 1989.

Grateful acknowledgment is also made to Princeton University Press for permission to quote material contained in the *Collected Works of C. G. Jung*.

And, of course, acknowledgment is made to the wonderful man (or men, or men and women) who wrote the Book of Revelation, without which this book would not exist.

Beginner's Guide to
Revelation

Figure 1. Even a "little book" of spiritual knowledge is too much for us to swallow; it tastes bitter unless it is shared. ("St. John the Divine eats the little book," Albrecht Dürer, first published in the 1948 edition of *The Revelation of Saint John*.)

CHAPTER 1

VISIONS OF THE MILLENNIUM

> Beginning with their Genesis, and carrying
> through their Old Testament of previous worlds,
> and their New Testament of the present to the
> Revelation of their esoteric ceremonialism, the
> tenets of this book are as sacred to the Hopis as
> the Judaic-Christian Bible is to other peoples.[1]

The world has grown so complex, so vague and ambiguous
that it sometimes seems beyond any individual's ability to
understand, much less control. The brave dreams of our Vic-
torian ancestors—convinced that they were on the verge of
solving all the mysteries and conquering all the demons that
had held us captive for so long—have grown stale and crum-
bled into dust. Once the theme of "progress" seemed an
anthem that would lead us forthrightly (and self-righteously)
into a glorious future of unending achievement; now
progress has stalled and our advance has yielded to retreat.
The mood has passed from optimism to pessimism, then to
despair and, most recently, to a greedy hedonistic apathy.

Yet on the horizon looms a sight so glorious and strange
that we don't even have mental categories to encompass the
vision. In one of Colin Wilson's books, he tells the story (perhaps apocryphal) of Captain James Cook's arrival in the
South Seas. When Cook's great three-masted ships appeared
on the horizon, the islanders could not see the ships. They
literally *could not see the ships* and were startled when the
white men appeared on their shores. Without some concept

---

[1] Frank Waters, *Book of the Hopi*. New York: Penguin, 1977, p. xi.

Figure 2. John's magnificent vision can be viewed as a "big dream" that tells us about a massive change of consciousness, in which humanity experiences the more than human contained within each of us. ("St. John's Vision of Christ and the Seven Candle Sticks," Albrecht Dürer, first published in the 1498 German edition of *The Revelation of St. John*.)

of such a ship, they could not find a mental compartment adequate for the strange sight before them, and so they saw nothing at all. Like the islanders, today we stare at visions that fill the field of sight and somehow manage to blank them out and see nothing at all.

All over the world, people are trying to contain these strange visions in some way. Change is never welcome, and when nothing but disaster is expected, all change appears to portend disaster. If the world isn't going to die of starvation, it will blow itself up. If the economic structure of the world isn't going to collapse, leaving the rich richer and the poor dead, then the reverse will happen: the undeveloped nations will become so powerful that the current world-powers will become second-rate has-beens. If the dictators don't get us, the terrorists will. We've heard so many terrible scenarios that we just sit numbly, expecting the worst. Yet all of these are just attempts to explain the previously unexplainable. When the familiar disappears, how else to try and explain the new?

All over the world, prophets are arising, reminding us of the old prophecies of world's end, or crying new prophecies to fit our times. All seem so close to our circumstances that we shiver and intellectualize them out of our sight, trying in our tired, frightened way to exorcize the demons that threaten to swallow us.

HOPI HISTORY

The Hopis first released information about their history, myths, legends, and religious ceremonies—all of which form a single entity for the Hopis—to Frank Waters, who published them in his *Book of the Hopi* in 1963. (In 1969, Waters published a more personal record of his time with the Hopis, and his difficulty in understanding the Hopi mind, in *Pump-*

Figure 3. The ancient prophesies of the Hopi Indians trace the creation and evolution of consciousness through "four worlds" (stages of consciousness) to date, and predict a "fifth world" in the near future. (Hopi Kachina from *American Indian Design & Decoration*.)

kin Seed Point.) However, the Hopis revealed only part of their mysteries at that time. More recently, they have chosen to release additional information through a variety of spokesmen, including members of other tribes, "breeds," and even whites. However, to understand the Hopi prophecies, we have to understand something of the Hopis.

The Hopis are an isolated, introverted, mysterious people, living alone on the plateaus of Arizona, surrounded by their numerous outgoing neighbors—the Navajos. Most anthropologists think that the Hopis were a Mongolian people who crossed the then-existent land bridge over the Bering Strait twelve hundred years ago, and then migrated southward. Tree-ring analysis shows that their three main settlements at Oraibi in Arizona were first settled over seven hundred years ago. The Hopis have lived there in their splendid isolation ever since.

The Hopis' own histories tell a very different story. According to Waters, they assert that they made a great ocean crossing, passing over a series of "stones" (i.e., islands), thousands of years ago. They didn't come from the North and migrate southward; they entered in Middle America and migrated northward. The medicine chief I studied with said that—in histories not revealed to Waters—the Hopis tell of the time before this migration, when an earlier migration was made—from the stars. They say that their ancestors came from the Dog Star Sirius one hundred and eighty thousand years ago. Interestingly, an African tribe with no known connection with the Hopis— the Dogon—also believe that their ancestors came from Sirius. The Dogon are also aware that Sirius has a "twin star" not visible to the naked eye, a fact not known to modern science until 1862.

In favor of the anthropologists' theory is the fact that every Hopi child is born with the Mongolian spot at the base of their spine, which seems irrefutable evidence that the Hopi, like their probable cousins, the Mayans, are Mongolian in origin. However, other evidence favors the Hopis'

version of history and argues that their Mongolian ancestors came to the Americas long before the land bridge
across the Bering Strait came into existence. For example,
fossil remains have placed people on the North American
continent over twenty thousand years ago. In addition,
analysis of blood groupings show that Native Americans
have the purest "Type-O" blood groups in existence. This
would mean that Native Americans were isolated from
their ancestors much longer ago than anthropologists
would have us believe. Frank Waters says:

> There is a great body of literature, ever growing
> from antiquity to the present, asserting that sea
> crossings were made from Asia to America cen-
> turies before the Vikings and Columbus arrived
> from across the Atlantic. The earliest of these is
> the most ancient Chinese classic, Shan Hai King,
> compiled about 2250 B.C. It describes a voyage
> across the "Great Eastern Sea" and a two-thou-
> sand-mile journey down the length of the land
> beyond. Long regarded as a book of myth, it is
> now asserted to be an accurate geographic
> description of various landmarks in America
> including the "Great Luminous Canyon" now
> known as Grand Canyon.[1]

WORLDS OF CONSCIOUSNESS

According to Waters, the Hopis' histories/mythologies talk
of four successive worlds, each destroyed by a great catastrophe, and after each catastrophe, people emerged into a

---

[1] Frank Waters, *Book of the Hopi* (New York: Penguin Books, 1977), p. 116.

new world. To the Hopis, the destruction of these "worlds" is—at one and the same time—both literal and symbolic. The "worlds" represent stages of consciousness and epochs of human history. At each stage, there is both a collective state of consciousness within the world and a corresponding personal state of consciousness within each person. We are now living at the end of the fourth world, which corresponds to the most material, the least spiritual, of the four worlds. It is the nadir; when it ends, a higher series of worlds begins.

According to Waters, after their "emergence" into the fourth world at the Tuwanasavi (i.e., Center of the Universe)—which is located at the current site of Hopi settlements in Arizona—the Hopis split into four groups or clans, and each went off to either the north, east, south, or west. Their task was to journey until they reached the sea, then return to their starting point. Having completed one "round," they would start in a new direction and again make a full round-trip. They were to proceed thus either clockwise or counterclockwise until they completed all four "rounds." Their journeys would have formed a great cross or swastika about the Tuwanasavi, where they could come together in a permanent settlement, free of clan arguments or differences.

They left pictorial records—glyphs—of their migrations on rocks throughout the Americas. Mayan glyphs can be readily read by Hopis, which supports the Hopis' claim that both had common ancestors. These pictorial records describe clearly how many of their four journeys each group had taken, and the order in which they were taken. Only the record at Oraibi, the home of the Hopi, shows all four migrations completed.

> The symbol found at Chichen Itza [author's note: the capital of the Mayan empire; a city which, like Babylon, became the capital of successive empires, each time to be abandoned and later

rediscovered] indicates that the people covered only one round before returning to the same area and attests to the Hopi belief that the Mayans were simply aberrant Hopi clans who did not complete their migrations.

The Emergence and the migrations are so beautiful in concept, so profoundly symbolic, one is tempted to accept them wholly as a great allegory of man's evolutionary journey on the Road of Life. It is difficult to reconcile a people having such an enlightened concept of spiritual life with an actual primitive people wandering over a vast and undiscovered continent in prehistoric times. Yet such were the Hopis. Archeological remains and ancient records attest this.[2]

HOPI RELIGION

Traditional Hopis live in isolation in Oraibi, shrinking in numbers, preserving their heritage, their magical teachings. They believe that by practicing their beliefs, they keep the world in balance (a 1983 movie *Koyaanisqatsi*, Hopi for "world out of balance," attempted to show the contrast between the balance of nature and the out-of-balance condition of modern humanity). They have no priesthood because every male Hopi serves as priest at one or another of their ceremonies during the year "after which he returns to work in his fields, wearing no vestige of priestly garb and carrying no aura of sanctity."[3]

---

[2] Frank Waters, *Book of the Hopi*, pp. 104, 115.
[3] Frank Waters, *Book of the Hopi*, p. 192.

The Hopis live a life so thoroughly entwined with religion that modern Westerners may have a difficult time grasping it. The Hopis view religion on both the abstract level and the literal level simultaneously, rather than falling into literalistic interpretation or dismissing religion with abstract interpretation. This combination seems—to Western eyes—either primitive or profound depending on our willingness to accept their very different view of reality. Linguist Benjamin Whorf studied the Hopi language and found that it exhibited the same complexity.

> . . . the Hopi thought world has no imaginary space . . . it may not locate thought dealing with real space anywhere but in real Space, nor insulate space from the effects of thought.[4]

That dual level of acceptance is most clearly expressed in their prophecies. The Hopis have studied these prophecies, which are spread over the walls of special underground chambers called *kivas* (literally, "world below"), sacred places where the Hopis hold their religious rituals. During the Hopis' ancient migrations, "they had no homes save small pits they dug in the earth and roofed over with brush and mud."[5] Like virtually everything else in the Hopi culture, these kivas evolved into both a practical solution to their need for a gathering place and a symbolic representation of their articles of faith.

> Cylindrical or rectangular, it was sunk deep, like a womb, into the body of Mother Earth, from which man is born with all that nourishes him. A small hole in the floor symbolically led down into the previous underworld, and the ladder-opening

---

[4] Benjamin Whorf, in E.T. Hall, *The Hidden Dimension* (Garden City, NY: Anchor Books, 1966), p. 92.
[5] Frank Waters, *The Book of the Hopi*, p. 126.

through the roof symbolically led out to the world above.

The kiva is thus the focal point of Hopi life. It abstractly symbolizes the tenets of the ancient ceremonies performed in it; it functions on the secular level; and it is the underground heart of all that is truly, distinctively Hopi.[6]

Others may visit many of the sacred sites of the Hopi—visitors frequently tour other more pedestrian kivas, but not these particular sacred caves where the ancient teachings are recorded. Like all such ancient knowledge, the prophecies are expressed in symbols and, hence, are open to interpretation, but the Hopi have had nothing but time to carefully study and interpret these writings. They were originally willing to withdraw into seclusion because the teachings told them that this would be necessary, that the white man would rule over the Indian for this long time.

THE TIME OF PURIFICATION

Several years ago, Michael Toms recently interviewed John Kimmey, a white man whom the Hopi elders picked to spread their message, on New Dimensions radio. Almost twenty years earlier, fresh out of the armed forces, Kimmey visited what he later found to be a sacred place in Northern California. While there, he experienced the earth "speaking" to him. He returned to the spot many times. During one visit, he "heard" two words: "Taos and Oraibi."[7] He

---

[6] Frank Waters, *The Book of Hopi*, pp. 127, 131.
[7] From the radio interview between John Kimmey and Michael Toms, New Dimensions Radio, Tape #1741, 1987.

vaguely knew Taos was a town in New Mexico, but had never heard of Oraibi, the village in Arizona where the Hopi Indians have lived continuously (in peace) for at least seven hundred years.

Kimmey went to Oraibi and told an elder there (a "grandfather" in Native American terms) his story. Then, in Taos he found the teacher he was intended to find: "Little Joe" Gomez, with whom he lived and studied for eight years. Upon Little Joe's death, Kimmey acquired a Hopi "grandfather." Since then, Kimmey has been both a student of the Hopi elders and a teacher of the Hopi children. He is an adopted Hopi and has been delegated by the Hopi to spread the Hopi prophecies.

In Kimmey's description of the Hopi prophecies, the time of "purification" (that is, the critical time of passage from one world to the next) would be announced by "a 'gourd of ashes' which is spilled upon the earth. This ash will be poison. Everything will burn for a great distance around that area and nothing will grow there for a long time. The ashes will get into the water and air. People who drink the water will soon die. Women who are exposed to it will not be able to give normal birth."[8]

In 1946, the first atomic test explosion took place in Almagordo, New Mexico. When the Hopis heard about the bomb, they knew this was the "gourd of ashes" which would announce the time of purification. In 1947, they convened a meeting of the elders of all the clans in Hopiland, in order to synthesize all their varied knowledge of Hopi teachings and prophecies into a single version they could present to the world, as their prophecies had told them they must. Though Frank Waters discusses none of this, it undoubtedly figured in the Hopis' decision to share some of their knowledge with him.

---

[8] Interview with John Kimmey, New Dimensions Radio, Tape #1741, 1987.

Kimmey says that the Hopis predict three great symbolic "shakings" of the Earth. The first is symbolized by the swastika, the ancient masculine symbol.[9] The swastika was also the pattern described by the migratory routes which the Hopis and Mayas took when they arrived in the Americas. The Hopi "grandfathers" interpreted World Wars I and II as the predicted "masculine" upheaval; the Nazi swastika was a proof of this interpretation. The Hopis saw these terrible wars as evidence of the trouble caused when the masculine principle, with its inherent need for aggression and expansion, is cut off from the gentle receptivity and containment of the feminine principle.

The second "shaking" of consciousness was symbolized by the Sun, which the Hopis regard as the symbol of the feminine because they view the Sun as the mother of the Earth. After much reflection, the Hopi "grandfathers" have concluded that the Western world's "continuing dialog with the Eastern hemisphere" (the land of the "rising sun") marks this second, feminine upheaval. Obviously, as evidenced by our wars in Korea and Vietnam, the West's response to the East has largely been negative. On the other hand, Japan's integration of Western ways into their Eastern culture marks a positive aspect of the dialog, as does the spread of Eastern fields of study such as Zen, Vedanta, Aikido, etc.

The third great shaking of the world is symbolized by the "red hat and red cloak people." They can either bring us wisdom that we accept, or they can destroy us. Kimmey says that "the Hopi people are very cautious about interpreting [this symbol] because we are in the midst of it."[10] A "purification" must inevitably occur, which will cleanse the remains of the "fifth world" to prepare for the "sixth

---

[9] The swastika is an ancient symbol that first appeared as early as the Bronze Age. Until adopted as the symbol of the Nazi party in World War II, it was an honored symbol with deep religious significance for virtually all early religious traditions except the Egyptians.

[10] Interview with John Kimmey.

world." (The "fifth world" occupies only a brief period following the longer four worlds discussed by Waters.) However, the symbol for the third shaking is ambiguously presented: either of two resolutions can occur. One possibility is a successful union of the male and female principles, which the Hopis view as following the inborn, instinctual plans set in each of us at birth by "the Great Spirit." The other possibility is, of course, that we can use the "gourd of ashes" to wipe out all life. If we take that path, the Hopis say that the world will be decimated in a single day, and "the ants" will be left to rule the world.

Happily, one predicted sign of the more positive resolution has already occurred. The Hopis predicted that the "red hat and red cloak people" would send a representative to share their wisdom with the Hopis. The Tibetan lamas—who wear red hats and cloaks—also have prophecies of the time of "purification." These prophecies say that "in the time when the iron bird flies and the iron horse rides on rails," the Tibetans would be exiled from their land and scattered over the earth. At that time, they must go to the place of the "red-faced people" to "plant the seed of the Dharma." Acting upon these prophecies, the exiled Dalai Lama asked his oracles where among the "red men" the wisdom should be taken; they said: "go to the Hopis."

Some time ago, a representative—Go Man Kin Rimpoche—was sent to Hopiland. The Hopi grandfathers asked if, in his trips among the various centers in the United States, he had seen any who had successfully merged the masculine and the feminine. Sadly, he said "no"; many were striving to join the two sides, but he concluded that cultural difference prevented the Americans from being able to successfully use the Eastern teachings. Despite this, the Dalai Lama still considered the Native Americans as offering the best chance of saving the world.

I'm reminded of the story Wordsworth tells of crossing the alps in his massive poem: "The Prelude."

Wordsworth and a friend went on a walking tour of the alps. Both looked forward with anticipation to the point when they would reach the peak of the alps. But their journey took them alternately up and then down so many times that they wondered when they would ever reach the top. They stopped a peasant and asked him how far it was to the top. He kept pointing back in the direction they had come from. Though there was some difficulty with language, they were finally made to understand "that we had crossed the Alps." The Hopis see the point of passage from the "fifth world" to the "sixth world" in similar terms.

SYMBOLS AND SIGNS

The Hopis are wise enough to understand that prophecies are symbolic. Unfortunately few in our materialistic times understand symbolism. We want something to be either true or false, with no shadings in between. We especially don't understand that something can be psychologically and spiritually true without being in any way literally true. We try and take a symbolic document, like the Bible, literally. That leads to two ridiculous extremes: (1) the scientist who condemns the Bible out of hand as nonsense because he knows that the world wasn't created in seven actual days, nor is it only 4,000 years old; or (2) the fundamentalist who accepts everything in the Bible as literally true even if it contradicts known historical or scientific facts. My mother heard a minister in her southern town say: "I believe everything in the Bible. If the Bible said that Jonah swallowed the whale, I'd believe it."

Much of religious works are the records left by someone who has had a great mystical vision into the heights or the depths of the spirit. Mystical visions are impossible to communicate rationally since there are no words adequate for the experience. However, since visionaries feel compelled to make an attempt at communication, they are forced to express the inexpressible in the only language possible—symbolism. The symbol system they use is normally common to their particular culture. That is, a Jewish mystic will communicate a vision in terms of Jewish religious symbolism; a Hopi shaman will communicate his vision in terms of Hopi religious symbolism.

Psychologist C. G. Jung said that a symbol is the "best possible expression at the moment for a fact as yet unknown." I will have much more to say about the nature of the symbol in the pages that follow. However, consider Jung's statement as a hypothesis in dealing with Hopi symbolism. Jung meant that a symbol cannot be reduced to any simple definition because it is prior to definition. Symbols come first, rational explanations come much, much later. As Jung never tired of stressing, a symbol is not a sign.

Though Jewish mystics and Hopi mystics express their individual visions in symbolism characteristic of their cultures, the underlying experience tends to be largely identical. Once the cultural trappings are removed, the underlying symbol is universal. That's why, for example, a conscious pastiche using symbols reduced to signs (which was a common literary mode in the Middle Ages) no longer engages our interest, while a true vision using seemingly identical symbolism still captivates us.

We all encounter similar symbols every night in our dreams. Both Freud and Jung realized that dreams, coming from the unconscious, were preverbal and spoke not in words, but in symbols. But Freud regarded symbols largely as empty signs. Long objects, for example, are phallic symbols; hollow objects symbols of the vagina. In contrast to Freud, Jung regarded dreams as sacred mysteries, each a window on both our personal unconscious and on a transpersonal realm he termed the collective unconscious.

Jung felt that a true symbol is inexhaustible. A cave in a dream might, in part, represent a woman's vagina. It might represent anything hidden away from consciousness. The symbol of a cave would carry all the connotations that caves have had, both in our personal lives and in the life of mankind. We might have visited one of the great caves, like the Carlsbad Caverns or Mammoth Caverns. We might remember Tom Sawyer's harrowing confrontation with Injun Joe in the cave. We might remember the Caves of Mirrabar in *Passage to India*. Each such experience of a cave would impart a particular resonance to our unique relationship to caves.

Hundreds of thousands of years ago, our ancestors lived in caves, protected against the terrors of the night. Tens of thousands of years ago, their first religious ceremonies were held in special caves, hidden from the knowledge of those not allowed into their mysteries. Two thousand years ago, the ancestors of many of us buried their dead in catacombs, holy places where at least in death they could be safe from persecution.

When we dream of a cave, all of those associations cluster around the symbol of a cave. The similarities and differences between our particular dream cave and all those other associated caves further color the symbol. The context in which the cave occurs in the dream, the dreams we have had before in which caves appear, everything adds to the richness of the symbol. It is just not sufficient to reduce a cave in a dream to a vagina.

For Jung, every person, every object, every situation in a dream is a symbol, capable of almost infinite amplification; that is, we don't follow a single associational string of memories back to a single source, nor do we say a cave equals a vagina and that's that. Instead, we build up a penumbra of associations, personal and transpersonal, that surround every part of the dream. The associations between each person, each object, each situation in the dream blur into each other, since ultimately every symbol can encompass all of human experience if it's stretched far enough.

Let's return to Jung's contention that a symbol is the "best possible expression of a fact as yet unknown." In our example, a cave occurs in a dream because there is something unknown which is being presented to our conscious minds from the unconscious—something for which we have no adequate verbal expression. This unknown something can be better expressed by a cave—a particular cave in a particular circumstance—than by anything else. Once we consciously understand the issue presented by the dream, it's no longer unknown; the unconscious no longer needs to present us with that particular cave.

THE COLLECTIVE UNCONSCIOUS

What is the source of these symbols which appear in the Hopi prophecies, in great religious works, in our daily dreams? In his studies of the dreams and fantasies of his patients, as well as in his readings of the mythologies of widely divergent cultures, Jung came to accept that each of us contains within us a doorway into a far wider world which he called the collective unconscious: "collective" because it is accessible to all, "unconscious" because it can't be reached through conscious awareness. It's a much maligned and much more misunderstood concept which we will refer to many times in these pages.[11] For now, the reader should be aware that material which comes from the collective unconscious has a vast amount of emotional energy; it is experienced as numinous, awesome, eerie, godlike, or any of the other human reactions to the more-than-human.

---

[11] For more discussion of Jungian concepts, see my book *Beginner's Guide to the Archetypes,* to be published by Nicolas-Hays in 1995.

The late Mircea Eliade, the 20th century's greatest religious historian, saw the world of myths and prophecies much as did Jung, but with a difference in emphasis. The great moments in the life of a person or a nation are all existential crises, times when no solution based solely on reason or tradition will do. These watersheds generate incredible energy because of our nearly total involvement in the issue, our inability to escape from the problem. At such times, this energy enables us to transcend our normal world and pass into the world of religion; we are forced by our desperate need to advance into a new relationship with divinity. Eliade argues that religion comes into existence at these "limit-points" of human experience.

Eliade sees the world of the collective unconscious accessible to the individual through dreams and visions as only one manifestation of the Godhead, and a limited one if it isn't actualized in the outer world. Thus Eliade sees the myth as more primary than the dream, because it was powerful enough to move many people, while the vision or dream of an individual moves only one individual at a time. Jung sees the dream as foremost, the myth its best attempt at collective expression. But both are far too aware of just how difficult it is to denote primacy to either inside or outside, individual or collective, when the gods play with the world.

BEYOND LINEARITY

Once we begin to think symbolically, we begin to live symbolically. We reject literal interpretation, we reject linearity. As I've mentioned earlier in this chapter, the Hopis' great migrations consisted of moving as far as they could go in one direction, then returning to their starting place, making a cycle or a round—thus circularity. Returning to the starting point, they turned at right angles and made another round. Four rounds made a cross, seemingly linear. Yet there was more; at the end of each arm of the cross, the Hopis took care to turn briefly at right angles before they retraced their path; thus the cross really formed a swastika. A swastika is an expression of the movement inherent in the seemingly linear; a swastika is ready to spin, forming a wheel. If this seems to be a complex system, please note that the Hopis are totally aware of this symbolism, and have refined it at great lengths in their elaborate symbol system.

> From one point of view the unconscious is a purely natural process without design, but from another it has that potential directedness which is characteristic of all energy processes. When the conscious mind participates actively and experiences each stage of the process, or at least understands it intuitively, then the next image always starts off on the higher level that has been won, and purposiveness develops.[12]

At a very difficult time in his early adult life, four years after breaking with Sigmund Freud (four years he spent in lonely isolation exploring the inner world of his dreams and visions), Jung had a great dream. This dream demonstrated that the developmental path each of us takes during his or her life (which Jung termed "individuation") is not linear. Instead, it can be best expressed by a spiral. A spiral is both cyclical and linear, thus much like the Hopis' swastika.

Visualize a spring resting on its base, coiling upward. Taking a godlike view, looking down on the spring from the sky, it looks like a single circle. Looking at it from the

---

[12] C. G. Jung, *The Collected Works of C. G. Jung*, trans. by R. F. C. Hull. Bollingen Series XX. Vol. 7. *Two Essays on Analytical Psychology* (Princeton, NJ: Princeton University Press, 1951, 1966), p. 386.

ground, it appears like a series of sloping lines, each separate and distinct, advancing into the sky. From the godlike view, moving around the spiral is just an endless trip around the circle, each time coming back to the starting point in a rather Sisyphean effort. However, from the ground, the movement seems to pass gently upward, disappear for a moment, then appear at a higher level, ready to begin another upward journey.

PSYCHOLOGICAL CONTAINERS

The important thing in viewing any prophecy is to resist the temptation to become lost in a useless examination of its literal truth. It's fascinating if both the Hopi and Tibetan Buddhist prophecies actually predicted the critical world events leading up to our present watershed. However, in this book, I'm going to be much more concerned with symbolic truth than literal truth. The Hopi prophecies speak symbolic truths about changes in consciousness. Prophetic literature of all cultures speak in symbols, symbols whose primary purpose is to capture inner—not outer—change.

If the symbols are accurate enough to show outer events as well, more power to them. But prophecies are records of inner experiences of transformations and transcendence. These experiences are more similar than dissimilar—regardless of the time, place, or individual identity of the person recording them. Thus, all are potentially available to serve as psychological "containers" during times of struggle and transformation.

In a time of major transition—a time like today—we can approach prophetic literature as potential "containers" for our own new vision of reality. This vision seems too strange to be directly perceivable; it has to be seen through symbolic lenses. We need to find images, stories, songs, poems, that awaken something both old and new inside us. We need symbols which capture something of this strange new time, so that we have some alternative to the endless litanies of gloom and despair. The new is frightening because it destroys the old. But the new is also a thing in itself, and needs to be seen as such, not merely as the destroyer of the old, the negation of the known.

The Hopi prophecies provide us with a guide to the new. But still, we aren't Hopis. I've stressed just how isolated and introverted the Hopis are, with a view of reality closer to relativistic physics than to contemporary Western culture. Their whole life is wrapped up around their religion and their prophecies in a way that Westerners can only shake their heads at. In *Pumpkin Seed Point,* Waters described how, after three years spent largely with the Hopis, he was as far from understanding them as he was when he began. The Hopi prophecies, while fascinating for all, can only serve as psychological containers for the Hopis themselves. But perhaps there are other prophetic books closer to us that will serve us as the Hopi prophecies serve the Hopis.

The Bible is the Western world's record of its spiritual teachings and prophecies. Though we may live in the late 20th century and many may believe that "God is dead," the stories, heroes, legends, and symbols of the Bible are so ingrained in our psyches that they still evoke wonder in nearly everyone. We may not be able to quote chapter and verse like our ancestors, but most know the Bible stories, often without remembering where they learned them. More importantly, even if we have never read the Bible, or heard it read to us, the Bible is part of our heritage, a heritage that is unique. The Bible can speak to those of us from a Western European heritage more directly than Hopi prophecies, or the Koran, or Buddhist Sutras.

In this book, I'll examine the Book of Revelation, the last book in the New Testament of the Christian Bible, and see if it can provide us with a container capable of capturing our unique time of transition.

PSYCHOLOGICAL TRUTHS
VERSUS LITERAL TRUTHS

The last major transition in consciousness began with the birth of the Christian era, the era of the god/human. Men and women began to realize that God wasn't exclusively outside, that we all contain divinity. Like the gods, we can think and create. When the Book of Revelation of the Bible was written (A.D. 1st to 2nd century) this new realization was still inchoate. It took nearly two millennia to rise to mass consciousness. Like other such prophetic documents, the Book of Revelation comes from deep places in the human soul. It speaks the symbolic language of dreams and visions, of myths and fairy tales. It is a perfect map for an approaching change of consciousness.

The Book of Revelation contains psychological truths about a change in consciousness. The energy generated in each of us by the symbols of the Book of Revelation is the purest proof that it is ultimately psychological "truth"; literal truth is not the province of this book. As Eliade never tired of demonstrating in his writing, religion is the separation of something from its environment in order to label it as holy. In Eliade's terms, the Book of Revelation is holy because we have singled it out as holy. My interest, like Jung's, lies in what that separation reveals about the psychological nature of transcendence. In examining a "holy" book in this manner, I have no intention of reducing it to the "merely psychological." I'm addressing the psychological truths it provides; its religious truths are the province of theologians.

Therefore, it is not to the point whether the Book of Revelation came into existence as a prophecy concerning the times when it was written, or whether it was a symbolic tool specifically created to guide an initiate into the deeper mysteries of Christianity, although there is a great deal of critical literature arguing for both points. It's not important to my study whether its author was one person or a series of people adding to and polishing oral and written sources (again there are arguments for both views).

The Book of Revelation has been all things to all people, a cornucopia of delight for scholars, theologians, crackpots, and madmen. It has never lost its magic power to arouse strong emotions; though we can read many contradictory meanings into its words, the words continue to fascinate. In fact, it is exactly because we can read multiple meanings into the words and images that they continue to fascinate us. All true myths and prophecies contain that more-than-human allotment of energy; they fascinate at a level not accessible to logical analysis.

This book is not an attempt to offer still another "true" reading of the Book of Revelation. I want to point out some of the symbols that still capture our attention, symbols that seem to speak to our times and our predicament. Whether this is why the words were written, and whether history will follow the pattern of this great book is not the issue. I hope we can be more like the Hopis and realize that prophecies speak more to the spirit than the flesh.

When something eternal in the human psyche speaks to us, the vehicle is not important. The only question is whether we can still experience the mystery of the revelation. If we come to prophetic material with the right attitude, we feel a chill run up our spine. Something deep inside us and, perhaps, atavistic, still experiences symbols directly, without the need for intellectual interpretation. And, if prophetic material is psychologically true, questions of literal truth or falsity are immaterial. When we approach the Hopis' teachings or the Book of Revelation, we need to listen with our whole being. The chill of recognition is important because these prophecies offer not only an end, but also a new beginning. The Book of Revelation doesn't end with Armageddon and the Fall of Babylon, but with the New Jerusalem!

CHAPTER 2

THE BEGINNING OF THE VISION

The Revelation of Jesus Christ, which God gave
unto him, to shew unto his servants things which
must shortly come to pass; and he sent and signified it by his angel unto his servant John:

Who bare record of the word of God, and of the
testimony of Jesus Christ, and of all things that
he saw. Blessed is he that readeth, and they that
hear the words of this prophecy, and keep those
things which are written therein; for the time is at
hand.[1]

The Book of Revelation is presented as a vision which
appeared to St. John ("the Divine" or "the Beloved," as he
is normally designated) on the island of Patmos, a small
island off the coast of Asia Minor near present-day Turkey.
I will use that convention in these pages even though most
scholars no longer believe the John of the Gospels to be
Revelation's author. I also won't go into any of the schol-
arly considerations about the document's history or interpretation beyond saying that it is a document most
probably composed in Greek between the first and second
centuries, A.D.

---

[1] The Revelation of St. John the Divine, 1:1–3. The Book of Revelation is
quoted from the King James version of the Bible. The full text of the
Book of Revelation is included in the Appendix.

A WORLD BEYOND TIME

In its original Greek, Revelation was crudely written, repeti-
tious, and grandiose, without regard for syntax or grammar.
This tends to be true of early versions of myths, fairy-tales, and
visions, just as it's true of the major dreams we have in our
individual lives, and is a sign that the version presented is a
true product of the unconscious, with less conscious manipulation than the more artistic versions that evolve later.

> I am Alpha and Omega, the beginning and the
> ending, saith the Lord, which is, and which was,
> and which is to come, the Almighty (1:8).

John describes a vision presented to him by God, but a very
special manifestation of God: a God who describes himself
as the "Alpha and Omega." Alpha and omega are the first
and last letters of the Greek alphabet. God as the alpha and
omega, the first and last, admirably captures the feeling of a
God beyond time, beyond beginnings and endings. That is,
this vision is to take place at a deeper level than more normal stories, like the timeless regions where fairy-tales
occur—"once upon a time."

The world of the unconscious is beyond time in just
such a way. We all know the difficulty of placing dream
events in any logical, linear fashion. Far too often in
dreams, events happen simultaneously, or seem to be connected, but have no logical connection whatsoever when
we try to reconstruct them afterward. Visionary experiences
are all of this sort. While mystics and prophets all speak of
the unity of their experience, they find it impossible to adequately describe that unity for others, because the experience is itself beyond limits or definitions.

> The conscious mind moreover is characterized by
> a certain narrowness. It can hold only a few

simultaneous contents at a given moment. All the rest is unconscious at the time, and we only get a sort of continuation or a general understanding or awareness of a conscious world through the succession of conscious moments. . . . The area of the unconscious is enormous and always continuous, while the area of consciousness is a restricted field of momentary vision.[2]

The world of the vision is not a conscious, logical, linear world. In John's vision, the alpha and omega is going to express concepts that go beyond limits of time, space, or cultural orientation. The Book of Revelation is commonly considered to be about the end of the world we know and the coming of the new world—the New Jerusalem. Yet, from the beginning we learn that this vision is beyond beginnings and endings. That is to say, words like beginning and ending mean something different in the vision than we commonly take them to mean. Because of our cultural background, most of us tend to think in linear terms, of a clear "start" and a clear "finish." We want goals, and we feel good if we make progress toward our goals.

The vision of John is not about the end of the world in any traditional terms. It takes place in a region beyond time and space that is the site of all religion, according to Mircea Eliade. The primary attribute of the collective unconscious is that it is beyond all our limitations of time and space. This is a world like the relativistic world of Einstein—the world of the time-space continuum—where neither time nor space has any intrinsic meaning, separated from the other. Similarly, the world of quantum mechanics is a world beyond time and space, where it is

---

[2] C. G. Jung, *The Collected Works of C. G. Jung*, trans. R. F. C. Hull, Bollingen Series XX, Vol. 18: *The Symbolic Life* (Princeton, NJ: Princeton University Press, 1976), ¶ 13.

possible to know either the position of a particle or its momentum, but not both.

Relativity and quantum mechanics—for all their seeming abstruseness—are merely attempts to accurately describe the physical properties of the world in which we live. Yet they seem to describe the same world that mystics encounter inside themselves. (Unfortunately for science, neither relativity nor quantum mechanics is able to adequately picture the unity that the mystic is able to directly perceive.) The world of the mystic is our world, and John's vision can tell us something about our deepest inner being at a time when we seemingly are about to move one full turn around the spiral (see chapter 1). From a godlike position, we will just be returning to where we began. But from our human perspective, we will be advancing to an entirely new level.

THE SYMBOLISM OF SEVEN

John to the seven churches which are in Asia: Grace be unto you, and peace, from him which is, and which was, and which is to come; and from the seven Spirits which are before his throne (1:4).

John is directed by God to reveal his vision to the "seven churches" of Ephesus (the major city of the area), Smyrna, Pergamos (or Pergamum), Thyatira, Sardis, Philadelphia, and Laodicea. These were all viable cities in that region at that time, cities with newly formed Christian communities. However, there were quite a few other such cities in exactly the same area: Hierapolis, Colossae, Miletus, and a half a dozen more nearby. Because of this, attempts by interpreters to make literal sense of why John addresses these seven churches and no others have fallen somewhat short of believability. In the vision, each city is addressed separately by God; each church has clearly distinguishable attributes. Therefore, I would suggest that it's the quality of "seven" that is important; we need to regard the seven churches as seven different states of mind, seven different ways of approaching transition.

The Book of Revelation goes out of its way to stress the symbolism of the number seven. John turns to see who told him to take the message to the seven churches. As soon as he turns, he sees:

> . . . seven golden candlesticks; And in the midst of the seven candlesticks one like unto the Son of man, clothed with a garment down to the foot, and girt about the paps with a golden girdle.

> His head and his hairs were white like wool, as white as snow; and his eyes were as a flame of fire; And his feet like unto fine brass, as if they burned in a furnace; and his voice as the sound of many waters. And he had in his right hand seven stars; and out of his mouth went a sharp two-edged sword: and his countenance was as the sun shineth in his strength (1:12–16).

In addition to the seven churches, there are seven candlesticks and seven stars. Helpfully, God, the alpha and omega, reveals the symbolic meaning of the sevens to John: "The seven stars are the angels of the seven churches; and the seven candlesticks which thou sawest are the seven churches" (1:20). Hence the Book of Revelation itself stresses that it is the "seven-ness" which is significant.

Read symbolically, these seven churches have represented many things to many readers. For example, some have stressed that there are seven Greek vowels beginning and ending with alpha and omega, which is an interesting coincidence. There were seven planets known to the ancients (a characteristic designation for the great thinkers of Greek and earlier times), which corresponded to seven types of personality or seven stages of the development of consciousness. There are seven energy centers in the body called wheels or chakras; these seven centers also correspond, like the planets, to seven stages of the development of consciousness.

> The significance of 7 in the Bible is fairly obvious; it means totality, fullness, completeness. At times it is multiplied by itself (7 × 7 or 7 × 70); this does not signify excess, but rather the removal of limit implied in totality. . . . The symbolism of 7 is extremely prominent in the Book of Revelation; there are 7 churches, lamps, stars, spirits, seals, trumpets, serpent heads, plagues, and other examples.[3]

To say only that seven signifies "totality, fullness, completeness" is to reduce it from a symbol to a sign. If it's a true symbol, it means all that and more. Perhaps the picture that most affects us here is that of the biblical God creating the world in seven days; i.e., the seven stages of creation, analogous to the seven planets and seven chakras. So, in this world beyond time (the world of the alpha and omega), a timeless God is going to speak to us of creation, where beginnings and endings are all contained together in some impossible balance.

If all that seems a little far-fetched, just ignore it for the present. I'm anticipating a little, since the messages of the Book of Revelation will be taught over and over again. In any case, next we'll see that the alpha and omega begins by giving the churches just the sort of practical, down-to-earth

---

[3] John L. McKenzie, *Dictionary of the Bible* (New York: Macmillan, 1965), p. 794.

advice that should lead us gently into the vision, as, of course, it is intended to do.

MESSAGES TO THE SEVEN CHURCHES

> I am Alpha and Omega, the first and the last: and,
> What thou seest, write in a book, and send it unto
> the seven churches which are in Asia; unto Eph-
> esus, and unto Smyrna, and unto Pergamos, and
> unto Thyatira, and unto Sardis, and unto
> Philadelphia, and unto Laodicea (1:11).

Each church has a particular sin, each a characteristic flaw in a time of transition to a new belief system, a new level of consciousness. In one town, Ephesus (2:1–7), the people no longer cling to a central belief; "thou hast left thy first love." But to those who overcome their fears and return to their deeper beliefs, "to him that overcometh will I give to eat of the tree of life, which is in the midst of the paradise of God" (2:7).

Another church, Pergamos (2:12–17), is composed of those who may hold to their beliefs inwardly, but are content to sit silently and watch as others do evil. The people of still another city, Thyatira (2:8–29), have listened to a false prophet (Jezebel) and followed her teachings instead of God's. The congregation of another church, Sardis (3: 1–6), with no hope for the future, chose to live only for the day and turned to dissolution. Another city, Laodicea (3: 14–22), in some ways the most condemned by the alpha and omega, is composed of the wishy-washy, the lukewarm, neither accepting nor rejecting anything anymore, content merely to go whichever way the wind blows.

Another church, Smyrna (2:8–11), is composed of those who are suffering greatly in these times, but manage to hold to their faith, even though others persecute them. They are already suffering martyrdom for their beliefs because of the sins of others in their midst: "the blasphemy of them which say they are Jews, and are not, but are the synagogue of Satan" (2:9). The alpha and omega reassures the faithful of Smyrna: Fear none of those things which thou shalt suffer . . . be thou faithful unto death, and I will give thee a crown of life (2:10).

However, only one city, Philadelphia (3:7–13), has fully satisfied God. The people there have never deserted their faith; nor have they yielded to dissolution. They have seen the new way opening before them and have already started to make a transition to the new. Therefore, alone among the cities, their people will not suffer and will not be exposed to temptation. (It was because of this biblical praise for the city of Philadelphia that William Penn named his newly founded American city: Philadelphia.)

Don't the attitudes of the seven churches sound like the attitudes of our day:

1) giving up our deepest beliefs, losing faith in our ability to deal with the difficult issues that confront us;

2) watching passively as others do evil, convinced we are powerless to control our destiny;

3) listening to "false prophets," willing to accept any false teaching just to avoid this terrible in-between state of transition;

4) turning to greed and sensuality, choosing to live only for the moment, since we see no future;

5) cowering in fear, too frightened to take a stand on anything, content merely to go whichever way the wind blows;

6) petulantly crying out against our fate, against the gods who have brought us to this pass?

Just as with the people of Philadelphia, some few have already seen the future opening up before them . . ."I have set before thee an open door and no man can shut it" (3:8). Those who are already stepping into this new state of consciousness need not fear, the alpha and omega tells them; so, too, for us. John's revelation is truly addressed to people with issues just like ours; he understands us! His revelation can serve as a teaching device to help us in this transitional period.

THE DEATH OF SELF-DEFINITION

> After this I looked, and, behold, a door was opened in heaven: and the first voice which I heard was as it were of a trumpet talking with me; which said, Come up hither, and I will shew thee things which must be hereafter (4:1).

Having addressed himself to our earthly condition, John now moves on to the great vision that will build, level by level, until we see the New Jerusalem rise before us. Remember that any vision from God, the alpha and omega, is beyond time. We will not see a sequential series of events, but rather a spiral of visions that attempt to take us deeper and deeper into a revelation which can't be reached directly. If one image doesn't strike us, another might. Having responded to one symbol, perhaps a symbol that earlier seemed meaningless will now resonate inside us.

John is transported to God's throne. Just to be sure that we won't forget that we are talking about a God of creation, beyond time, he is addressed as "him that liveth for ever and ever" (4:10) . . . a God "which was, and is, and is to come (4:8) . . . a God who "hast created all things, and for thy pleasure they are and were created" (4:11). God holds a book in his right hand. This book is sealed and: ". . . no man in heaven, nor in earth, neither under the earth, was able to open the book, neither to look thereon (5:3).

We are not able to open such a book in life because we are each limited by self-definition. To the extent that we say who we are, what and where we are, we have pre-

Figure 4. Jung discovered that the alchemical operations corresponded
to stages of the individuation process. For example, in the *solutio*, we
dissolve into our constituent parts in order to find a "solution" to our
seemingly "insoluble" problems. ("The Alchemist's Oven," Woodcut
from *Mutus Liber*, 1677).

cluded being able to see beyond that definition. We are blinded to the new, as the South Sea islanders were blinded to Cook's ships, because our old definitions are not sufficiently broad to include the new. But, in God's world, a world beyond definition, there is no such limitation. It is in just such a fluid state that we will find the answers we need, not in the rigidity of all the "certainties" about the world we live in.

Next there appears a "Lamb as it had been slain" (5:6). This lamb is able to take the book which "no man in heaven, nor in earth, neither under the earth, was able to open" (5:3), and open the great seals.

The lamb was the great early Christian symbol for Christ, later to be largely subsumed under the images of the fish and the dying and resurrected God. This is a "Lamb as it had been slain." Thus the Christ image we are concerned with in the Vision, the Christ who can open the Book, is the Christ who has already died as a sacrificial lamb. It is the dying which frees Him from definition, and enables Him to open the book.

So our first lesson in dealing with this strange world that John presents to us is that we have to die in order to fully experience it. John is allowed to see God's world in his vision, but death is the prerequisite for the actual experience. This theme of death leading to new life is one of the great themes of Christianity, as it was of the many other mystery religions. Christ had to die before He could be reborn, to be reborn before He could once again ascend into heaven. These terrible times, when death hangs around us like sackcloth, do not presage physical death, but a death which is inseparable from rebirth. There can be no creative process without death, and who among us any longer thinks that the world can continue along its same tired path, without some creative solution?

When definition dies, we are free to dissolve into our constituent particles. It is in that fluid solution that we will find the solution to our seemingly insoluble problems. But something has to die in order for that to happen. That something is the part of us which knows just who we are, where we live, what the world we live in is like, and on and on. It seems like a simple thing to give up that certainty, but most of us no longer realize that there is anything left of us if we strip away all those external definitions. We are afraid that there will be "nothing" left; that's the death of which we are all so afraid. But, of course, it is exactly "nothing" which we need to discover. Six hundred years before Christ was born, Lao Tzu taught this.

> Thirty spokes share one hub. Adapt the nothing therein to the purpose in hand, and you will have the use of the cart. Knead clay in order to make a vessel. Adapt the nothing therein to the purpose in hand, and you will have the use of the vessel. Cut out doors and windows in order to make a room. Adapt the nothing therein to the purpose in hand, and you will have the use of the room. Thus what we gain is Something, yet it is by virtue of Nothing that this can be put to use.[4]

Or if that seems too hard to accept, we might remember Alice's conversation with the king about "nobody."

> "I see nobody on the road," said Alice.
> "I only wish I had such eyes," the King remarked in a fretful tone. "To be able to see Nobody! And at that distance, too! Why, it's as much as I can do to see real people, by this light!"[5]

---

[4] Patrick Hughes and George Brecht, *Vicious Circles and Infinity: an Anthology of Paradoxes* (New York: Penguin, 1978), p. 55.
[5] *Vicious Circles and Infinity*, p. 55.

We're all afraid that when we strip off our conventional awareness, we'll find there's "nobody" left, "nothing" inside. But it is just that "nobody" we need to find, that "nobody" who is our essential self.

CHAOS THEORY

Science has recently had to confront a similar problem. Science is based on an analysis of cause and effect. Scientists look at some natural phenomenon; e.g., the motion of the planets in their orbits. They gather data about the phenomenon; e.g., the positions of a planet with respect to the sun at different times, and the mass of the planet and the sun. Having gathered that information, the scientist attempts to see a mathematical pattern in the raw information. If so, they formulate a hypothesis of what the pattern of behavior is. Using that hypothesis, they predict further behavior; in our example, the position of the planet at some future time. And, in cases like our example, scientists have been extraordinarily successful in extracting these patterns.

However, increasingly in the 20th century, scientists have come up against natural phenomena that don't yield their patterns so readily to observation and analysis; e.g., the weather. Scientists presumed that predicting weather patterns accurately was only a more complex version of predicting the positions of the planets. It was more complex because there were more variables. That is, the movement of the planets is such a massive undertaking that it can only be affected measurably by a very few things: the position of the planet from the sun, the mass of the two, and to a much smaller degree, the positions and masses of the other planets in the solar system. Interestingly, when more variables enter the picture, the predictions get much less accurate: e.g., in calculating the motion of a moon of a planet instead of the planet itself, since a moon is small enough that now both the sun and the planet have to be considered. (In fact, scientists have never been able to fully define even the relative positions of three mutually interacting planets. This is called "the three-body problem.")

However, inherent in science has always been the assumption that one can at least observe as accurately as possible and find an approximate pattern. Then better observation and the consideration of more variables will further improve the prediction. The fact that we've never been able to successfully predict the weather over long periods of time was just considered to be a temporary setback because we didn't yet have the tools to consider a sufficient number of variables accurately enough.

In his book *Chaos: Making a New Science,* James Gleick describes how the computer changed all that. In the early 1960's, meteorologist Edward Lorenz decided to set up a simple computer program with a small number of variables to model a simplified version of the weather. He would feed in numbers that defined the original state of the system and let the computer grind out a pattern of the weather changing across time (or at least the primitive version of the weather described by his program). He also let the computer draw a graph of the numbers so he could get a quick visual weather summary. One day he got lazy and decided not to bother to feed in the original set of numbers. He just picked up the numbers at a point midway in the previous day's run and started his program there.

After the program had chugged away for an hour or so, he was shocked to find that the graph looked absolutely nothing like the graph at the same point the previous day. At first, he figured that he had made a mistake and entered the wrong numbers, but that wasn't so. In trying to figure out what had happened he became the first to discover what has come to be called "Chaos Theory."

He found that no matter how accurately he recorded the numbers which supposedly described the state of his weather model, they were of necessity different than the original because of the limits of observation. That is, if his system was capable of handling twenty decimal places, anything beyond twenty decimal places was impossible to measure. According to traditional science, based on cause and effect, that would just mean that Lorenz's new pattern wouldn't be quite exact in matching the original pattern. What he found, instead, was that (in the prescient words of 19th-century mathematician Henri Poincare): "it may happen that small differences in the initial conditions produce very great ones in the final phenomena."[6] In other words, no matter how carefully you observe nature, your observations are never going to be good enough to predict nature. Eventually nature is going to fool you and come up with something totally unexpected, seemingly out of nowhere.

This understanding could be seen as sounding the death knell for science, but gradually scientists have begun to find instead the beginnings of a new science. In this new science, order can give way to chaos or seeming formlessness unpredictably. However, this chaos in turn yields to a new order. Thus chaos is a necessary step in the development of any force in nature, any organism, any system. A higher order of organization can't be produced by a simple extrapolation from the situation as we know it. Nature has always understood this truth: death is a necessary part of life. The old has to die in order for the new to be born. From the perception of the old, death is to be avoided at any cost. From the perception of someone up above the issue, death is just one further step in the development of the organism.

THE FOUR HORSEMEN

And I saw when the lamb opened one of the seals, and I heard, as it were the noise of thunder,

---

[6] Henri Poincare, 1903, *Science and Method* (Mineola, NY: Dover Publications, reprint 1952).

Figure 5. We live our whole lives riding on one steed or another. Unless we can learn to rein them in, to move at a canter or a gallop at our command, we can never have any real freedom. The four horsemen mark our ability to master those steeds during four progressive stages of our life: childhood, youth, adult and death. ("The Four Horsemen of the Apocalypse: War, Hunger, Plague and Death," Abrecht Dürer, first published in the 1498 German edition of *The Revelation of St. John*.)

one of the four beasts saying, Come and see. And I saw, and behold a white horse: and he that sat on him had a bow; and a crown was given unto him: and he went forth conquering, and to conquer.

And when he had opened the second seal, I heard the second beast say, Come and see. And there went out another horse that was red: and power was given to him that sat thereon to take peace from the earth, and that they should kill one another: and there was given unto him a great sword.

And when he opened the third seal, I heard the third beast say, Come and see. And I beheld, and lo a black horse; and he that sat on him had a pair of balances in his hand.

And when he had opened the fourth seal, I heard the voice of the fourth beast say, Come and see. And I looked, and behold a pale horse: and his name that sat on him was Death, and Hell followed with him. And power was given unto them over the fourth part of the earth, to kill with sword, and with hunger, and with death, and with the beasts of the earth (6:1–8).

As the lamb opens the first four of the seven seals on the Book, he releases—one at a time—four horsemen—the fabled Four Horsemen of the Apocalypse. We live our whole lives riding on one steed or another: desire, love, fear, hatred, greed, ambition, power. All carry us where they want, not where we want. Unless we learn to rein them in, to make them move at a canter or a gallop at our command, we can never have any real freedom. Of all the meanings which the Four Horsemen carry for us, let me suggest the most famous: the white horse carries the inno-

Figure 6. Psychologically, death represents a state of transformation where an old attitude has to die in order for a new, broader view of life to emerge. ("Death" [detail], Gustave Doré, first published in *La Sainte Bible*, 1860.)

cent child; the red horse the impetuous youth full of his own power. The black horse carries the adult with his careful scales: weighing life, judging it. Finally, as the vision tells us directly, the rider on the pale horse is death!

Once again, the vision repeats a theme we will hear many times: we must pass through death before we can advance to new life. Each of the steeds is powerful, and we all know those who never progress beyond one or the other of the four. Each rider sneers at the others, but none recognizes his own limitations, nor the need for all four modes of travel. The child sees everything afresh and can't even imagine the concept of death. Yet, as Wordsworth said: "The child is father of the man." Youth, reveling in his power, mocks the ingenuousness of the child. Yet without that naivete, the dreams of youth quickly yield to the practicalities of the adult world.

The adult, able to hold his desires in check, looks askance at the license of youth. Yet without youth's passion, reason slowly cools into death. Death, seeing the vanity of all worldly pursuits, despairs of the adult, who weighs the values of life as if they had any real worth. Yet death, in its tomb of meaninglessness, needs exactly the definition that the rational world of the adult provided. Only one who has passed beyond all four, like the lamb, can reveal deeper mysteries.

> And when he had opened the fifth seal, I saw under the altar the souls of them that were slain for the word of God, and for the testimony which they held (6:9).

The opening of the fifth seal releases those who died for the word of God; that is, we are now dealing with just those who have passed beyond the child, the youth, the adult, beyond death itself. These are those who have made an analogous journey to that of the lamb.

THE SIXTH SEAL

And I beheld when he had opened the sixth seal, and, lo, there was a great earthquake; and the sun became black as sackcloth of hair, and the moon became as blood;

And the stars of heaven fell unto the earth, even as a fig tree casteth her untimely figs, when she is shaken of a mighty wind.

And the heaven departed as a scroll when it is rolled together; and every mountain and island were moved out of their places.

And the kings of the earth, and the great men, and the rich men, and the chief captains, and the mighty men, and every bondman, and every free man, hid themselves in the dens and in the rocks of the mountains (6:12–15).

Clearly the time is approaching in the vision when all earthly things must pass away. But first there is a pause while the angels of God put God's seal on the twelve thousand chosen of each of the twelve tribes of Israel (chapter 7:1–17). Just as the vision already taught in the instructions to the seven churches, those who are already "chosen," by virtue of seeing and accepting the new won't suffer during the transition. The hope is that all of us who read the Book of Revelation will discover our own door into the future, in order that we won't have to needlessly suffer.

As before, the cause of the suffering is too sharp a self-definition, an inability to change. The new only causes pain if one can't—or won't—give up the old, or can't tolerate the paralyzing state of chaos that intervenes between the old and the new. It is just the "great men" of the existing world—those who are too strongly defined within the terms of that world—who have to descend into darkness before they can come up reborn. They, too, have to give up their old definition.

With the opening of this sixth seal, the world as we know it comes to an end. Just as God created the world in six days and rested on the seventh, the seventh seal marks the hiatus between worlds, a time of chaos which we, stuck in the old mold of being, can only experience with "fear and trembling."

SUMMARY

Before we pass on to the revelation produced by opening the seventh seal, which begins a new cycle—and the description of this cycle occupies over two-thirds of the entire Book of Revelation—let us take stock of what we have already seen.

The vision has been presented to us as a story beyond time; i.e., we are not talking about history but about mythology. Mythology is the deepest level of our experience of the world, so the mythic answer to our dilemma is very important. Just so that we won't think that the author of the Book of Revelation is speaking of some purely personal mystical vision far from the world we live in, the vision starts with instructions to seven actual churches. The people in these churches are experiencing much the same problems as we are today, and are responding just as we are responding. The advice given them is so down-to-earth, yet so uplifting, that it gives hope that the vision may offer some answer to our problems.

Having provided that grounding, John proceeds to describe his mystical vision of what the transitional stage will be like. The fate of our world is contained in a book that can only be opened by a Christ who has died as a man, and freed himself from the definitions of who, what, and where which we mistakenly consider to be our identity. The book he opens has seven seals; six will concern the world, and the seventh will form a bridge toward a new world.

The first four seals show us the four stages of life: the child, the youth, the adult, and death. The fifth seal reveals that those who can pass beyond these four stages won't suffer in the transition period. The opening of the sixth seal begins to bring the existing world to an end.

Image after image has already been used to try to demonstrate in different ways that John's vision takes place in mythic time, and to demonstrate the need to die to the old life in order to be reborn into the new. These same themes will be addressed in many other ways in the remainder of the vision. However, from this point on, the nature of the transition phase and still later the vision of the glorious New Jerusalem to come will also begin to occupy more of the vision.

CHAPTER 3

THE NATURE OF ORACLES

> Every process is partially or totally interfered
> with by chance, so much so that under natural
> circumstances a course of events absolutely con-
> forming to specific laws is almost an exception.[1]

When we arrive at the seventh seal, we come to the end of a
cycle, and begin a new one. Each group of seven in the
Book of Revelation leads to another group of seven, creating an inward spiral, intended to take us ever deeper into
the mysteries. This idea of a group of seven as a full cycle,
with the seventh member of the group having a different
character than the first six, is beautifully expressed in a
hexagram called "Return" in the ancient Chinese book of
wisdom, the oracular *I Ching*. But before we discuss the
concept expressed in "Return," we must take a detour in
order to try to understand the nature of the *I Ching* and
other oracles (such as crystal balls and tarot cards, palm
reading, etc.). For oracles and visions are closely related;
both occur at the boundary between conscious and unconscious, order and disorder, or as Mircea Eliade calls it, "the
sacred and the profane."

---

[1] C. G. Jung's foreword to Richard Wilhelm's translation of the I Ching,
p. xxii.

THE *I CHING*

The *I Ching* consists of descriptions and commentaries on sixty-four hexagrams that are intended to correspond to every major human or cosmic condition. *Hex* is Greek for the number six; hexagrams are thus diagrams composed of six lines. Each oracle has a different character, a character that conforms to the culture which gave rise to the oracle. The *I Ching* is very much a wise old Chinese gentlemen, preaching patience and moderation. More than any of the other oracles, it can also be abrupt and pointed, especially when one is asking to be allowed to enter a course of action one already knows to be wrong.

The *I Ching* is traditionally consulted by casting yarrow stalks. One picks up the stalks randomly and then goes through a prescribed procedure to cast off stalks until one has narrowed the possibilities down to four situations: yang, yin, old yang, old yin. Yang is written as a solid line, yin as a broken line. "Old yang" means yang which is so yang it is about to change into its opposite—yin. Similarly, "old yin" is a broken line which becomes a solid line. "Old yang" and "old yin" are called "moving lines" because they are "moving" into a new situation. Thus, four states of the yarrow stalks correspond to each of the four symbolic states—two stable, two in motion.

Yang and yin represent two very elementary divisions of reality that are hard to capture in Western thought. Usually, they are considered to represent masculine and feminine, and that expresses them perfectly if we appreciate that masculinity and femininity aren't necessarily synonymous with male and female. This split into masculine and feminine is the basic polarity expressed in the mythologies of all cultures, and is, of course, highly determined by each culture's experience of the masculine and the feminine. However, there is also a sense of the union in opposition that passes beyond any cultural experience, that is beyond human experience at all. The Chinese are clear about that when they discuss yang and yin; they describe them as containing all polarities: masculine/feminine, active/passive, positive/negative, creative/receptive, hard/soft, and many, many more.

Usually today, the random toss of three coins is substituted for the random sorting of yarrow stalks, again to arrive at one of the four possibilities. There are two sides to a coin; therefore, there are eight (i.e., 2 × 2 × 2) possible throws of three coins. One corresponds to "old yang" (say 3 heads); one to "old yin" (say 3 tails). Two tails and one head would mean "yang"; two heads and a tail "yin." Thus, of the eight possible combinations, one is "old yang," one "old yin," three are "yang" and three are "yin."

HOW 64 BECOMES INFINITY

The coins are thrown and the lines written from bottom to top. After six throws, there are six lines making up the final hexagram. Since each line can be either yang or yin, there are sixty-four hexagrams altogether (i.e., 2 to the 6th power = 2 × 2 × 2 × 2 × 2 × 2 = 64). Together these sixty-four hexagrams form a total picture of reality at any desired level, from the personal to the cultural to the cosmic; the commentaries on the lines recognize this multi-leveled ambiguity and move easily between all three.

Since any of the lines can be either "stable" or "moving," any hexagram can change into any other hexagram. This corresponds to a view that any situation in life can change to any other situation. As in life, true stability is unlikely, but possible. Mild change is more likely, but a drastic change where every line changes into its opposite is also possible, though unlikely.

Since any line can be both stable or moving as well as yang or yin, the *I Ching* really expresses not 64 possibilities, but 4,096 possibilities (i.e., 4 to the 6th power). The philosophy behind the *I Ching* is wise enough to recognize that these are not independent possibilities. Rather, they are the total possibilities which lie within a smaller number of general situations. Each of the hexagrams represents such a general situation: "peace" or "conflict" or "difficulty at the beginning" or "enthusiasm," to name just a few. The particular moving lines represent the possibilities within a general situation which make it unique for any particular question.

Consider how we usually attack a problem. We ask ourselves if we should do this or that; we consider possible but opposing solutions. If the problem is more complex, we subdivide each of these possible solutions into two more. Perhaps we are complex enough to do this a third time, but that is probably beyond what any of us actually do with real problems in our lives. Well, the *I Ching* does that six times in an attempt to broadly represent any situation which can occur in either our individual lives, in the lives of societies or cultures, or even in the life of the universe which surrounds us. It is a profound concept. Jung expressed it this way:

> Western man is held in thrall by the "ten thousand things;" he sees only particulars, he is ego-bound and not thing-bound, and unaware of the deep root of all being. Eastern man, on the other hand, experiences the world of particulars, and even his own ego, like a dream; he is rooted essentially in the "Ground," which attracts him so powerfully that his relations with the world are relativized to a degree that is often incomprehensible to us.[2]

---

[2] C. G. Jung. *The Collected Works of C. G. Jung,* trans. R. F. C. Hull, Bollingen Series XX, Vol. 12: *Psychology and Alchemy* (Princeton, NJ: Princeton University Press, 1953, 1968), ¶ 8.

Of course, even 4,096 situations are not sufficient to handle the enormous number of possibilities even a single life presents, much less the possibilities within a culture, or within the universe itself. The *I Ching* extends from 64 situations to 4,096 by the addition of moving lines. The 4,096 become immeasurably large by the addition of the particular situation a questioner brings to the *I Ching*. There is the question itself, the total personality of the questioner, the culture in which the questioner lives, and so on. That creates an infinite system between the questioner and the oracle.

Because of its nearly infinite (possibly actually infinite) ability to structure reality, the *I Ching* adapts readily to different users. A Jungian analyst friend, for example, would only throw the *I Ching* under exceptional circumstances. When at one key time in his life, he was in bad straits and threw "Waiting," he then waited over a year before he threw again (that's almost unimaginable for me). He threw Waiting again and waited still another year. He told me sadly that he thought he would probably he on his death bed, consult the *I Ching*, and get Waiting.

Jungian analyst Marie-Louise von Franz says that she never goes anywhere or does any significant action without consulting the I Ching. Jung himself looked not only at the lines that he threw, but the other lines of the hexagram as well. He wanted to remind himself of the complete possibilities available within the particular hexagram he had thrown (remember that any hexagram can change into any other hexagram by the proper combination of moving lines).

CONSTRUCTING OUR OWN REALITY

Now one explanation for why oracles work ("constructivists" would claim it to be the only explanation) is that the human mind can't tolerate unstructured material.

Given chaos, the human mind will impose a structure, and, of course, that structure is predetermined by the possibilities available within a given individual's mind. In addition, the structures are limited to those things which any human can conceive of, and further limited to those things conceivable by a person in a particular culture in a particular time.

Beyond that, there is the question of whether collective structures are available which go beyond those acquired within a given person's lifetime. Jung, and I, would argue strongly that there are such structures: the archetypes of the collective unconscious. We would argue further that they far and away outnumber an individual's personal memories, to the same degree that the life experiences of all people who have ever lived (and at still deeper levels in the unconscious, the life experiences of all creatures who have ever lived) greatly outnumber the experiences of a single person. Though many would totally deny the existence of any such "collective unconscious," most would accept that humans have some inborn mental structures which limit the possibilities of mental experience.

To enable this structuring capability to come into play, oracles all provide a number of identical elements. First, the answers an oracle provides have to be ambiguous enough that they can fit many different situations. That gives the mind free rein to put whatever interpretation seems appropriate onto the oracle's answer. This is exactly analogous to the way that Jung felt that archetypes operate. Jung insisted that archetypes have structure but no particular form; they take their form from the particular situation. This is another way to say that the human mind operates through symbols: ambiguous structures that, in Jung's already several-times-repeated words, "are the best possible expression at a given time for something as yet unknown."

Across time, the human mind accumulates symbols (which Jung calls archetypes) which help it structure experience. Across time, cultures accumulate symbols which help structure experience and record them in oracular systems. In working with oracles, the symbol-making characteristic of the human mind combines with a parallel set of symbols recorded within the oracle to produce meaning.

Note that ambiguous does not mean gibberish for either the archetypal symbols of the collective unconscious or the recorded symbols of oracles. The great oracles have a second characteristic: they are highly concentrated repositories of human wisdom. If the answers provided by an oracle ran against human experience, the oracle would be ignored; there would be no match between the symbolic operation of the human mind and the symbols provided by the oracle.

PREDICTING THE FUTURE

If the reader has paid close attention throughout this extended discussion on the *I Ching* and other oracles, he or she will have noticed that virtually everything we have said about why oracles do what they do could equally have been said of John's vision and of other prophetic material, like the Hopi prophecies. Perhaps it seems a little strange to relate one of the greatest religious prophecies of the Western world to an Oriental "fortune-telling device" (as most Westerners would regard the *I Ching*). But both oracles and prophetic visions are attempts to predict the future by extracting information from the timeless world of the unconscious and structuring it through symbolic systems of thought.

The collective unconscious seems to have no practical limits in time or space. But future time does seem different than past time. Sometimes it appears whole and complete at some earlier time, exactly as it will happen later. But more usually, it appears to be projected out of the totality of information already accumulated; projected in some organic way, like an oak tree can already be seen in an acorn if one knows how to look carefully enough.

This difference corresponds to our best scientific knowledge of how the human brain deals with sensory experience. In the 17th century, philosopher John Locke first made some attempt to deal with the relationship between the mind and the world. He said that the human mind was a blank slate on which sensory experiences were recorded. Sensations were viewed as separate and discrete little particles, much like the separate and discrete particles that made up the then revolutionary Newtonian concept of the physical world. Those discrete sensations were recorded on the blank slate of the human mind, available to be recalled as necessary. Our thoughts were nothing more than linear strings of these sensations, much like pearls strung on a necklace. The brain was a passive receptacle for sensory data.

Just as Locke drew on Newtonian physics for a physical analogy, 19th century philosopher John Stuart Mill drew on chemistry (the great science of the 18th century). Mill proposed that ideas were not just linear combinations of sensory experiences; rather they were "compounds" much like chemical compounds. That is, a new thing formed when the sensory units were combined in the right combinations at the right time.

In the 20th century, scientists for the first time began to study the way the brain operated. As a simplification, it was proposed that sensation led directly to response in a straightforward arc. This is the model which behavioral psychologists still use. By the 1950s, it was clear that the situation was more complex. It was discovered that not only did information from the sensors lead to the brain, information from the brain led to the sensors. A "feedback" model was proposed where the sensory information not only led to a response, but was also fed to the brain. The brain makes a comparison with information previously stored, then sends back the result of the comparison to the sensors as a corrective factor. Thus, at any time, the response is determined both by the sensory information being fed to it, and by corrective information from the brain.

This evolved into a more efficient "feedforward" model where the brain was continually "predicting" the required future response in advance of receiving sensory information. The brain did this on the basis of both sensory information it had just previously received, and its stored memories of responses to similar sensory information. Rather than the brain correcting incorrect responses to sensory input, the sensors led to corrective behaviors. The brain became much more active than passive.

Thus we live continuously in the future! Our brains are continuously projecting the future from the past, and feeding that information to our sensors. We proceed on the basis of that extrapolated future unless the sensors note some discrepancy which has to be dealt with. This seems to correspond exactly to what we know of the operation of the collective unconscious. It is continually drawing on past experience in order to feed forward its best estimate of the future. At any given moment in time, the collective unconscious is composed of all the experiences of the past, all that is going on presently anywhere among humans, and organic projections into the future based on the first two components.

However, we find ourselves at a unique point in history. Very soon, we will reach the point where there are more people alive in the world than have lived and died in all previous ages put together; as one radio sage put it: "the dead will become a minority." I believe this shift is the same as the shift which we have been discussing throughout this book. As long as past experience vastly exceeded current experience, the collective unconscious was inherently conservative: ritual and structure outweighed novelty. Archetypes changed so slowly as to seem eternal. When current experience exceeds past experience, the situation reverses: novelty and change reign supreme. Archetypes should come into existence in dizzying numbers, many staying around too shortly to register. But some stable new archetype, some "living symbol," should emerge in an astonishingly quick fashion (by comparison with the glacial scale on which archetypes normally emerge), an archetype powerful enough to overwhelm the archetypes created by the entire past experience of mankind.

In this book, I am arguing that we are going through a major change in consciousness at this unique moment in history. In fact, I feel that we are going through not a major change, but *the* major change. Later in this book I will present the Bible as a record of the development of consciousness, and Revelation as the culminating point in that development.

THE TURNING POINT

At last we have arrived at "the turning point." One of these sixty-four hexagrams (#24 in the usual ordering scheme of the *I Ching*) is called "Fu." Richard Wilhelm translates "Fu" as "Return" or "The Turning Point" in his classic translation of the *I Ching* from which I'll be quoting below. This hexagram captures exactly the unique nature of the cycles of seven that we experience in the Book of Revelation and throughout the Bible. Hexagram "Fu" says that:

> All movements are accomplished in six stages,
> and the seventh brings return. Thus the winter
> solstice, with which the decline of the year begins,

comes in the seventh month after the summer solstice; so too sunrise comes in the seventh double hour after sunset. Therefore seven is the number of the young light, and it arises when six, the number of the great darkness, is increased by one. In this way, the state of rest gives place to movement.[3]

The *I Ching* is saying that all things grow to a peak, then decline until they reach a state of "great darkness." When the darkness can grow no further, the "young light" appears again to start a new cycle. By the time of the opening of the sixth seal in the Book of Revelation, the "great darkness" has grown in John's vision and the seventh seal will once again produce a "young light," it will start a new cycle. But nothing ever fully repeats; spring may reoccur every year, but every year it is different, because the world is different.

So this new cycle, beginning with the opening of the seventh seal, will teach us the same lessons taught in the first cycle in different ways. If we have already learned these lessons in the first cycle of seven, we will learn them now at a deeper level. If we haven't yet grasped the point of the lessons, then perhaps this new cycle will give us an image which will free our minds sufficiently for us to advance past the place where we are blocked. Once that happens, we can return to images that previously seemed nonsensical, and now grasp their meaning. I'm sorry to keep belaboring this point, but not many of us think any way but linearly, starting at the beginning and proceeding steadily to the end. But the world of myths, dreams, and visions is a timeless world—the world of the unconscious—where linearity is abolished, since linearity is only a construct of consciousness.

---

[3] Richard Wilhelm, translator, *The I Ching*, Bollingen Series, XIX (Princeton, NJ: Princeton University Press, 1977), p. 98.

It's important to remember that John's vision takes place in the unconscious. While there is no linear progress in the unconscious, each trip into the unconscious should be undertaken in order to increase consciousness. One journeys into the "great darkness" of chaos in order to find the "new light" of a new order.

> Differentiation is the essence, the sine qua non of consciousness. Everything unconscious is undifferentiated, and everything that happens unconsciously proceeds on the basis of nondifferentiation—that is to say, there is no determining whether it belongs or does not belong to oneself.[4]

We come to a time of transition because we have grown too rigid, too set in our ways. In the unconscious, there is no definition at all. As long as we hold on to our rigid self-definition, we experience ourselves as lost in a formless world. If we are great heroes, like John is, we "die" to self-definition and experience the unconscious not as formless and undefined, but as a single great unity which goes beyond normal definitions. When we emerge from the unconscious, it is impossible to retain that unity in the world of polarities we live in. Hopefully we can retain enough to see the world with new eyes. It then becomes the job of consciousness to make new discriminations not available within our old rigid patterns of definition.

.

---

[4] C. G. Jung, *The Collected Works of C. G. Jung*, trans. R. F. C. Hull, Bollingen Series XX. Vol. 7: *Two Essays on Analytical Psychology* (Princeton, NJ: Princeton University Press, 1953, 1966), ¶ 329.

CHAPTER 4

THE APPROACH OF DARKNESS

And when he had opened the seventh seal, there was silence in heaven about the space of half an hour. And I saw the seven angels which stood before God; and to them were given seven trumpets.

And another angel came and stood at the altar, having a golden censer; and there was given unto him much incense, that he should offer it with the prayers of all saints upon the golden altar which was before the throne. And the smoke of the incense which came with the prayers of the saints, ascended up before God out of the angel's hand.

And the angel took the censer, and filled it with fire of the altar, and cast it into the earth: and there were voices, and thunderings, and lightnings, and an earthquake. And the seven angels which had the seven trumpets prepared themselves to sound (8:1–6).

Let us return once more to the vision. When the seventh seal is opened by the lamb, "there was silence in heaven about the space of half an hour" (8:1). In other words, there is a short pause to mark the end of the cycle, the "turning point," before there is a "return" to a new cycle. After this short pause, seven angels with seven trumpets appear, clearly inaugurating a new cycle of seven.

As you will recall, the opening of the first four seals represented the world as we know it, through the symbols of the four horses of the Apocalypse, each symbolizing in part one of the four stages of life. Similarly, in this new cycle, as each of the first four angels sounds their trumpet, the vision will address concerns of the mundane world, but in some new way, in order to once more attempt to produce the shock of recognition in each of us.

The first angel sounded, and there followed hail and fire mingled with blood, and they were cast upon the earth: and the third part of trees was burnt up, and all green grass was burnt up.

And the second angel sounded, and as it were a great mountain burning with fire was cast into the sea: and the third part of the sea became blood; and the third part of the creatures which were in the sea, and had life, died; and the third part of the ships were destroyed.

And the third angel sounded, and there fell a great star from heaven, burning as it were a lamp, and it fell upon the third part of the rivers, and upon the fountains of waters; and the name of the star is called Wormwood: and the third part of the waters became wormwood; and many men died of the waters, because they were made bitter.

And the fourth angel sounded, and the third part of the sun was smitten, and the third part of the moon, and the third part of the stars; so as the third part of them was darkened, and the day shone not for a third part of it, and the night likewise.

And I beheld, and heard an angel flying through the midst of heaven, saying with a loud voice, Woe, woe, woe, to the inhabiters of the earth by reason of the other voices of the trumpet of the three angels, which are yet to sound (8:7–13)!

As we see, each time an angel sounds his trumpet, one-third of some part of our world is destroyed. Consider what that might signify. Our normal day is divided into three parts:

1) eight hours of waxing sun;

2) eight hours of a waning sun; and

3) eight hours of darkness.

Most Western people have eight hours of work, eight of play, and eight of sleep. The eight hours of sleep, that third of a day of darkness, is sharply distinguished in our minds from the two-thirds of a day of waking and light. We try not to think of that time of darkness and dreams. We pretend that we don't dream, or if we do, that the dreams are meaningless.

Yet nightmares leave us all shaken and afraid. We are not so modern that we can laugh at our nightmares as they are happening, and dismiss them as silly phantoms of the night. Nightmares are too powerful for that. Nor are we so "enlightened" that we can laugh at nightmare's shadowy daytime companions: panic, anxiety, depression. It's only in the safety of light that we can dismiss the darkness.

The third of our life governed by darkness is always there, waiting to be addressed, asking patiently for an answer to its endless question. Shakespeare's Hamlet phrased the question as: "to be or not to be." But we all ask ourselves in some way: "What is the meaning (the hidden meaning) of my life?" Since that question is too painful, we try to depersonalize it and instead ask: "What is the meaning of life" (just *a* life, not *our* life), as if we can separate ourselves dispassionately from the issue. And, running still further from terrors of the night, some modern philosophers called logical positivists have tried to reduce the question to a linguistic riddle, a question that signifies nothing. But the night cannot be dismissed so easily.

So the first four angels bring the concept of darkness more directly into our lives; they insert a third of a deeper darkness, the darkness of the void, into every part of the world. The world of earth and plants is split into light and dark by the first angel (8:7). The second imposes this disintegration on the sea itself, the source of life (8:8–9). The third onto all the fresh water, hence into the water that forms us (8:11). It is as if—recognizing that we are a product of the sea—the angels first attack our relatively new home—the land. Then they destroy first the sea without, then the sea within. They leave no place for us to evade the darkness, no den where we can crouch concealing our fear. The point is most pronounced with the fourth angel. His trumpet splits darkness and light themselves into darkness and light, a deeper darkness and, by contrast, a deeper light (8:12–13).

CANTOR'S SET

Think of the first four angels as taking away the middle, leaving only the extremes. In such a world, every issue becomes polarized, split into opposites. No connecting links remain; no common ground is left to resolve any problem. Everyone and everything is isolated, alienated. This is the apotheosis of the modern world as presented us by Nietzsche, by Kierkegaard, by Kafka. Surprisingly enough, we can find a counterpart to this situation in modern mathematics, of all places.

In the *fin de siecle* period in Western Europe, when so much else was changing, German mathematician Georg [sic] Cantor was rethinking the nature of infinity. Cantor was successful in his attempt to place a measure on the mathematical concept of infinity. In doing so, he discovered or clarified many of the anomalies that lie within the infinite. For example, contrary to common sense, he proved that there are exactly as many even numbers (i.e., 2, 4, 6, 8, 10 . . .) as there are countable numbers (1, 2, 3, 4, 5, 6 . . .). In fact there are as many fractions (1/2, 1/3, 2/3 . . .) as there are countable numbers.

If the reader doesn't believe this, just consider what we mean when we say that, for example, we have exactly as many fingers as we do toes. Don't we mean that we can match each toe with exactly one finger? We don't care in what particular order we match them, but every finger has to match with one, and only one, toe.

To prove that there are exactly as many even numbers as countable numbers, Cantor said to match each countable number (1, 2, 3 . . .) with the even number that was twice as big as itself (2, 4, 6 . . .). Now there are no countable numbers left unmatched because—for any countable number—Cantor could tell you which even number it matched with. For example, 587 would match with 2 × 587 = 1,174. Going the other direction, if you named an even number, he could tell you which countable number it matched with merely by dividing it by 2. Every countable number matched with one, and only one, even number. Cantor argued that, therefore, there were the same number of even numbers as countable numbers. Quite a puzzle, and one that was inherent in the nature of infinity.

You could also match every countable number with every number that was a multiple of three, using exactly the same technique. Or for that matter, match every countable number with every number that is a multiple of a million, or a billion, or anything you like. But note that each of the sets is still infinite; that is, there is no final number that is a multiple of two, or three, or a million, or a billion, or any other countable number. If the reader doubts that, just imagine that there is some biggest number which is a multiple of three, for example; let's call it 3N. Then add three to it (i.e., 3N + 3). The new number is bigger than the biggest number, yet still a multiple of three (i.e., 3N + 3 = 3 times (N + 1). So there is an infinity of numbers which are multiples of three (or of a million, a billion, etc.).

In general, Cantor proved that we could match the set of countable numbers with every infinite subset of itself. However, not all infinities turned out to be the same size. Cantor was able to prove that the infinity of points on a line was of greater magnitude than the infinity of countable numbers; hence the number of points on a line is termed uncountably infinite. None of Cantor's discoveries about infinity was stranger than that which mathematicians have termed the Cantor Set.

Imagine a straight line stretching out to infinity in each direction. Further imagine that an infinitely sharp knife (that is, a knife whose blade has no dimension at all) cuts the line at two places, thus separating off a "segment" of the line from the rest of the line. There is an endpoint at each end of the line. Mathematicians term a segment of a line closed if it includes both endpoints. Cantor took a closed segment of a line and removed the middle, leaving two closed segments. Then he took the middle out of each of those two segments, leaving four closed segments. He continued this process infinitely; i.e., no matter how small the line segments, he kept taking out the middle.

It is hard to imagine what could be left after such a process; in fact, what is left is very strange indeed. First, there are an uncountably infinite number of such line segments. That is, there are as many such segments as there are points of a line. Yet, second, they are all "discontinuous." By "discontinuous," mathematicians mean that things are separated from each other. More precisely, for any two points, you can prove that there is a separation between them, a void.

This seems to be an exact counterpart to the situation created by the first four angels. The language of this chapter of the Book of Revelation goes out of its way to demonstrate that the angels take a third out of everything, right down to lightness and darkness themselves. From Cantor's Set, we are able to see what is left: an "uncountably infinite" world where everything is separated from everything else. This is the ultimate in alienation and a brilliant prelude to the supra-mundane world that is to follow.

For example, consider that perhaps John is picturing a world where we can no longer feel any assurance of the reality of everything we have previously taken for granted. Until the modern world of electric lights, day and night were worlds as separate as if they were on different planets. Now John is saying that right in the middle of day, you'll find night; in the middle of night will be day. The implication is that this separation continues indefinitely just as it does in Cantor's Set: each little piece of day has a middle filled with night, and each piece of night a center of day, no matter how deeply you dig.

This is similar to what is presented as the most basic symbol of Chinese philosophy: the yin-yang symbol. There a circle is divided into a light half and a dark half by an S-shaped curve. Within the light half is a dark circle, within the dark half a light circle. The point is again that there is no light so bright it doesn't contain its own darkness within, no dark so black it doesn't contain light at its core. Just so, each of us contains darkness within, a darkness with which we will have to come to terms, for within the darkness is a new light. In order to do so, we have to confront our fears, accept our alienation and find a bridge to the new.

FIRE AND WATER

There are other instructive details contained in the description of the destruction caused by the first four angels. The first angel brings a rain of hail and fire mixed with blood

(8:7). Hail is solid water, destructive water. Blood is usually regarded as a mixture of fire and water because it's warm with the energy of life. So the vision is already addressing mixtures of the seemingly incompatible.

The second angel's trumpet marks the fall of a volcano into the sea, changing the sea itself into blood (8:8). Thus once more fire is mixing with water. Once more blood is the result, but this time the whole sea is blood. The third angel's trumpet notes the fall of the star "Wormwood" into the earth's rivers (8:10–11). A star is solid, contained fire. Now it's fire that's solid and then mixes with water.

We use the description fire and water to signify opposites which bristle on being brought together. It's an opposition of equals. Fire can heat water to the point where it transforms and turns into steam and hence into air. Or water can put out a fire, extinguishing its natural process of transformation, reducing it to the solid which was burning. Clearly, when fire and water are brought together, no one knows the result. Something will inevitably be destroyed in the process, a process of transformation.

When "Wormwood" falls into the rivers, they turn bitter; when people drink the water, they die. Thus the volatile combination of fire and water is more than we, in our stability, can absorb. Just as fire can "kill" water and water can "kill" fire, the combination kills the person who tries to contain it. To bring that somewhat down to earth (as was the point of bringing the star from the heavens), consider fire and water as expressions of human experience.

The Greeks (and, in fact, many other ancient cultures) said that all nature was composed of four elements: earth, air, fire, and water. In human experience, water corresponds to our emotional nature, especially our softer emotions: sorrow and pity, bathed in the water of tears. Fire shows our volatile nature, filled with anger, aggression, passion. When sadness and anger come together inside us, it is usually more than any of us can handle. We feel totally torn apart from within; we "bleed." As stable creatures, we're just not up to reconciling such opposition within ourselves. So we "die"; that is, we give up our definition of who we are, and are transformed. And of course, it's to achieve that transformation, that "change of personality," that we struggle with the unconscious forces within us, and with the unconscious forces projected by mankind out onto the world.

> Continual conscious realization of unconscious fantasies, together with active participation in the fantastic events, has, as I have witnessed in a very large number of cases, the Act firstly of extending the conscious horizon by the inclusion of numerous unconscious contents; secondly of gradually diminishing the dominant influence of the unconscious; and thirdly of bringing about a change of personality.[1]

SUMMARY

The first four angels, like the first four seals of the Book of Life in the previous cycle, have addressed the world as we know it. The sounding of their trumpets brought together the irreconcilable opposition of fire and water, darkness and light, destroying the possibility for gentle compromise. Their actions took out the middle of everything, the shared middle that made the world connected and whole. They left the pieces of the world strung together like the elements of "Cantor's Set": uncountably infinite in number, yet each separated from one another. However, this doesn't have to be the final story. Beneath the seeming separation is a deeper unity.

---

[1] C. G. Jung, *The Collected Works of C. G. Jung*, trans. R. F. C. Hull, Bollingen Series XX. Vol. 7: *Two Essays on Analytical Psychology* (Princeton, NJ: Princeton University Press, 1953, 1966), ¶ 358.

Each time in the vision the first four of anything (seals, trumpets, etc.) take us progressively farther into separation and alienation within the mundane world we all live in. Then the fifth breaks through the mundane into the deeper world that lies beneath, a world in which there is no separation. Thus we know that the sounding of the fifth angel's trumpet will usher in deeper mysteries of the world beyond, the world where a greater unity can form, just as the opening of the fifth seal released those who had already transcended life and death.

CHAPTER 5

JUNG'S ANSWER TO JOB

There was a man in the land of Uz, whose name
was Job; and that man was perfect and upright,
and one that feared God, and eschewed evil (Job
1:1).

THE BIBLE AS A HISTORY OF CONSCIOUSNESS

This book argues that John's vision records the stages of a
transformation from one level of consciousness to a new
higher level of consciousness. But the entire Bible can be
interpreted in a similar fashion, as a complete history of
consciousness recorded through the stages of development
in the relationship between mankind and God. The part of
that history recorded in the called Old Testament (that is,
the testament before Christ) begins with God's creation of
man in Genesis (of which we will have more to say in chapter 8) and ends with the tiresome fulminations of Yahweh in
Malachi. In Malachi, God is reduced to ranting and raving
that no one honors him sufficiently. He is insistent that: "I
am the Lord, I change not." Proud words coming just before
the total change from the Old Testament God to Christ.

The story of Job (along with its poetic companions
Psalms, Proverbs, Ecclesiastes, and the Song of Solomon)
stands at the midpoint of the Old Testament, between
essentially historical records of the old and prophesies of
the new. Thus Job is the fulcrum, the pivot between an

Figure 7. The vision forms a series of seven-fold spirals as it progresses: seven seals, seven trumpets, etc. In each case, the first four stages correspond to the mundane world, the next two to the deeper world within, and the seventh to the passage to still another seven-fold spiral. ("The Seven Trumpets," Albrecht Dürer, first published in the 1498 German edition of *The Revelation of St. John*.)

older state of consciousness represented by Yahweh, and a new stage of consciousness, represented by Jesus Christ. (I'm indebted to Edward Edinger for this realization, which he pointed out in his book, *The Bible and the Psyche*).

The New Testament is the record of Christ and his followers. It records a different form of God, a God who struggles with the combination of divinity and humanity. He suffers, dies, returns from the dead, then removes himself back to heaven, away from the world of mankind. At that point, nothing is left for us but to take on Christ's mantle and repeat his struggle within our own twin nature.

Revelation is the last book in the New Testament of the Bible. It stands as a bridge between the record of the Bible and the unknown times ahead. It is a vision rather than a history, because it records a stage of consciousness which cannot yet be actualized in reality. It's a dream of what might come to pass and the necessary stages of that passage. It was written at roughly the same point in time as the Gnostic heresy of Abraxas. Both are attempts to capture a new stage of consciousness which was then just beginning to form, but which has now reached a saturation point.

Jung was fond of making an analogy between the formation of symbols in the unconscious and the formation of crystals in a saturated solution. The process is instructive. Take sugar, for example, and thoroughly dissolve it in water—you may have to heat it. Add more sugar and slowly dissolve it as well. Keep up this process of dissolving the sugar. Eventually the water will reach a saturation point; that is, no more sugar will dissolve. If a single grain of sugar is then added, it will gather other grains about itself into a crystalline structure particular to sugar. In the blink of an eye, the glass of water will become filled with a solid mass that seems to have no relationship to the solution of water which was there before. Perhaps one little grain of wisdom from John's vision will serve to form a new symbol where before there were none.

Figure 8. Jung viewed the developing relationship between human and God in the Bible as a record of the evolution of consciousness. The story of Job marks the first point when an individual is able to confront God with a moral dilemma. From that point on, it becomes inevitable that Christ will appear, and that humanity will realize its essential divinity. ("Job and his Friends," Gustave Doré, first published in *La Sainte Bible*, 1860.)

JUNG'S BREAK WITH FREUD

Jung struggled with similar issues to those presented in the Book of Revelation. His struggle led him initially to a "channeled" book that discussed the Gnostic god Abraxas. At first, he didn't understand that material at all. However, over time he integrated it into his life and incorporated it into his books in a more understandable fashion. Late in his life, it led him to a new understanding of Job's struggle with God, an understanding that humanity had a role to play in God's own development. Because this is so central to the point of the book you're reading, we need to follow Jung on that journey.

It began at a time when Jung, too, left the mundane world behind. From 1906 to 1912, Carl Jung had a close and complex relationship with Sigmund Freud. Freud considered Jung his "favorite son" and designated him to be his successor. However, the price Jung had to pay for this honor proved too high; he had to accept Freud's views uncritically. In particular, Jung felt that Freud's reduction of all dream symbols to sexual images was a terrible impoverishment of the rich palette of dreams. To Jung, dreams were mysteries of never-ending fascination rather than simple rebuses.

In 1906, psychologist Theodore Flournoy published a volume of the dreams and fantasies of a female patient referred to as "Miss Frank Miller." Jung considered this an ideal vehicle to analyze since the dreams and fantasies were filled with material Jung considered to be "collective"; that is, not part of Miss Miller's personal history. In 1912, Carl Jung published *Symbols of Transformation,* in which he interpreted "Miss Miller's" material. Instead of toeing the Freudian line of reducing dream images to sexual interpretations, Jung's interpretations drew extensively on mythology to amplify the collective images. Jung traced her psyche's attempts to re-establish psychic wholeness.

Freud considered Jung's publication of *Symbols of Transformation* a heresy against the Freudian dogma, and "excommunicated" Jung from the then small body of psychoanalysts. Jung had admired Freud deeply and found his exclusion a painful isolation. But he decided that if he was right, and Freud was wrong, then he would have to explore the unconscious forces within himself no matter where they took him. Therefore, he began a personal journey into the realm of his own unconscious dreams and fantasies, a journey which parallels the journey John is taking in his revelation.

This turned out to be a dangerous journey, but one that Jung survived, and drew on for knowledge and support in the years to come. In the course of this exploration, he discovered collective personified forces within his own psyche just as he had found collective images in "Miss Miller's" fantasies. However, having abstract knowledge of something is a much different thing than experiencing it oneself. In this inner struggle, Jung found that the unconscious forces were powerful enough to shake his personal consciousness to its roots.

A GHOSTLY PRESENCE

After more than three years of this struggle, toward the end of his personal confrontation with the unconscious, Jung felt the stirring of something new forming both within and without. He said that he felt that "the air was filled with ghostly entities." This atmosphere permeated his whole household. One Saturday morning in 1916, one of his daughters reported seeing a ghost; independently, another daughter told her parents that she had felt her blanket snatched away twice in the night. His son had a strange numinous dream which he painted the next morning.

Then on Sunday afternoon, the front doorbell began ringing, though no one was at the door. This went on for some time. The whole household, including two maids, listened to the ringing and even watched the doorbell moving in and out, with no one pushing it. As Jung said: "The atmosphere was thick, believe me!"

Jung felt the ghostly presences crowding around him, and went to his study to write. As soon as he began, the atmosphere lifted. In three evenings, he produced a very strange little book called *The Seven Sermons to the Dead*, ostensibly written by the second century Gnostic philosopher, Basilides. The writing was florid and grandiose—a style Jung found intensely embarrassing—certainly as far from his previous dry, academic style as could be imagined.

The material—if it could be understood at all by a modern reader—was equally far from Jung's previous clinical writings. It spoke of fullness and nothingness, of unity in polarity, of hierarchies of gods, of the relationship between gods and men. It spoke of many things that meant little to Jung at the time, but would come to mean a great deal at a later time.

THE GNOSTIC HERESY

True to its supposed Gnostic author, *Seven Sermons* contained what might be regarded as the primary Gnostic heresy; that is, the belief that the God of light and goodness, the God of Christianity, is co-equal with the God of darkness and evil, the Christian devil. Beyond those paired Gods was a further God—Abraxas—who surmounts all polarities: light and dark, full and empty, good and evil, etc.

Jung only distributed the book among personal friends, and later regretted having released it at all. In many ways, it contained the germ for all of his later writings, but in a form

few if any could understand. Today this book would probably be called "channeled" material. Most present-day "chan-
nels" are content to serve as passive conduits for supposed
higher powers—sometimes wise men from the past, sometimes aliens, sometimes strange energy sources. In contrast,
Jung viewed the material as a deep and important personal
message to him from the unconscious, a message with which
his conscious mind had to deal. He spent the rest of his life
struggling with this message from the unconscious, trying to
"consciously" integrate the "unconscious" material.

I believe that such channeled material is becoming
more common because the communication between the conscious and unconscious is becoming more common. Jung
invented a technique of extending dream work, called
Active Imagination, which he described as follows:

> . . . Take the unconscious in one of its handiest
> form, say a spontaneous fantasy, a dream, an irra-
> tional mood, an affect, or something of the kind,
> and operate with it. Give it your special attention,
> concentrate on it, and observe its alterations objec-
> tively. Spare no effort to devote yourself to this
> task, follow the subsequent transformations of the
> spontaneous fantasy attentively and carefully.
> Above all, don't let anything from outside, that
> does not belong, get into it, for the fantasy-image
> has "everything it needs." In this way, one is cer-
> tain of not interfering by conscious caprice and of
> giving the unconscious a free hand.[1]

Fritz Perls, the originator of Gestalt therapy, developed
many analogous techniques for bridging the gap between
consciousness and the unconscious. For example, if a patient

---

[1] C. G. Jung, *The Collected Works of C. G. Jung*, trans. R. F. C. Hull, Bollingen Series XX. Vol. 14: *Mysterium Coniunctionis* (Princeton, NJ: Princeton
University Press, 1955, 1956), ¶ 749.

was having difficulty resolving some conflict with her mother, Perls might use his "two chair" technique: the client would sit in one chair with an empty chair opposite her. She would imagine her mother in the other chair and tell her all the things she wanted to say, but never could. Then she would move to the chair of her mother, "become her mother" and answer from her mother's point-of-view. If the reader has never been involved with such therapy, it may sound like empty play-acting. It isn't! People can fall into this so thoroughly that emotional revelations of enormous consequence result from this seemingly simple technique.

Perls used a similar technique to help a patient understand a dream. She would talk to some person or, better yet, object, in the dream. This sounds like it is even less likely to work than the "two-chair" technique, since at least there the patient has some understanding of the person placed in the other chair. Seemingly they know nothing about the object from the dream. How could an object have any personality anyway?

But it operates just as strongly. The object was placed in the dream by the unconscious. When the patient talks to the object, it is the unconscious that answers, and it can provide a great deal of information that wasn't presented in the dream. Of course, the patient may feel silly during the process and may refuse to let the unconscious speak. However, it is always surprising to people new to this technique how strong and autonomous the voice of the unconscious is.

Try using Jung's Active Imagination technique in a similar fashion to Perls' use; that is, engage in dialog with the unconscious, either out loud, or at a word-processor. It is important to record these dialogs, so that consciousness can engage further with the unconscious material. Sometimes the voice is of incredibly more power than normal. This is a mark that it is coming not from a person's personal unconscious (the residue of personal memories and information), but from the collective unconscious. When the personality is a product of the collective unconscious, one finds virtually nothing of one's own personality to latch onto. It is as if one was visited by the gods.

It's difficult to separate channeled material from visions such as John's. Both undoubtedly come from the same timeless region—the collective unconscious. Both speak of the eternal truths known only in that region, in the grand manner of speech appropriate for such matters. Perhaps ultimately the only distinction is in the material itself. If you'll recall from our discussion of symbolism in chapter 1, Jung said that a symbol was the "best possible expression at the moment for a fact as yet unknown."

In the great mystical visions, such as John's, the symbol perfectly captures a problem confronting a whole epoch in time. In lesser channeled material, that perfection is lost, and the grand becomes merely grandiloquent. In Jung's own case, the original visionary material—though it contained virtually all of his later work "in embryo"—was inadequately captured in its original expression; instead Jung had to integrate it into his life and into his writings over nearly forty years.

Jung was lucky enough to have his vision when the time was ripe for its symbolism to be consciously expanded and understood. Eighteen hundred years earlier, when John had his vision, it was too early for conscious realization. The fact that we are—in small part—now able to amplify his vision in the book you are reading, demonstrates that the time may finally be ripe.

ANSWER TO JOB

Now we have to move forward thirty-five years in Jung's life. Jung is 75, and has completed nearly all his great works (only his magnum opus *Mysterium Coniunctionis* remains to be published and it is nearing completion). In the midst of a feverish illness, Jung once more feels that pressure from the unconscious, the pressure of something unformed trying to be born. Once more, he takes up his pen and begins to write; the pressure eases, the illness lifts.

But this time, the material, which he called *Answer to Job,* was written in a simple, human fashion, rather than in the florid language of the unconscious. After nearly forty years of searching for a rapprochement between conscious and unconscious, Jung no longer had to merely serve as an unconscious conduit for channeled material. The unconscious material could be integrated into his consciousness and then be translated directly into purely human terms.

If this sounds unusual, another incident from that time in Jung's life might lend it some credence. Jung had a great respect for the *I Ching,* which he had discovered through the translation of his good friend, Richard Wilhelm (whose translation was used in our discussion of the *I Ching* in a previous chapter). Throughout the years Jung used the *I Ching,* he invariably found the answers to be both apt and profound. However, in late life, he was discussing the *I Ching* with his younger colleague, Dr. Marie-Louise von Franz. Jung remarked—somewhat sadly—that he could no longer use the *I Ching.* She asked why, and he told her it was because he always knew what it would say. In other words, his conscious mind was so in contact with the unconscious—which the *I Ching* and other "oracles" draw on—that such intermediate tools were unnecessary.

Answer to Job is an answer to the question which the story of Job presents the reader: how can God be so unfair in his treatment of this just man? How can a God who is all good allow evil to flourish in the world? Traditional Christian theology views evil as an "absence of good," hardly on the same level with good. As we have seen, *Seven Sermons* already revealed the Gnostic heresy that the Christian God of goodness and light was merely co-equal with the Christian devil of darkness and evil. Beyond this God was a further God—Abraxas—who contained all such polarities within his unity. In the person of Jehovah, this was the God encountered by Job.

Job's story contains the most sustained poetry in the Old Testament, and is the only biblical work written in dramatic form. To recall briefly the story of Job, God was discussing the blameless character of Job with his servant, Satan. Satan tells God that it's easy enough to be faithful when you're favored by fortune, as Job is. He warns God that things would be otherwise if Job wasn't so fortunate. As Jung points out, hearing Satan's words, God behaves like an insecure tyrant who is only too ready to believe these slanders against his faithful servant Job.

God allows Satan to torment Job in order to see if Job will remain faithful. And torment him, Satan does. Job loses everything: his health, his wealth; even his children are killed. And, finally, he does rail against God's injustice—in Jung's view a sound protest. Three fatuous friends try to assuage his bitterness with homilies, but he dismisses their arguments as beside the point. Job knows that he has behaved well, yet been treated shoddily. He wants justice. But to whom can one appeal for justice from an unjust God?

Job appeals to God! In other words, at the same time that God is treating him unjustly, Job also feels that God will judge the situation fairly. As Jung points out, the only way this position could make any sense at all is if God were a multiple being, at one and the same time both just and unjust. In other words, Job is appealing not to a God of goodness and light, but to a God, like Abraxas, that contains all opposites.

However, Job receives little justice. Instead God terrifies the poor man further, parading his infinite power like some insecure overlord might. As Jung stresses, the disparity between their relative positions is so extreme that the idea that God needs to further humiliate Job is absurd. God reveals himself to Job not as the God in whose image man was made, but as the inhuman god who made the leviathan, the behemoth. This is not a portrait of a God of goodness and light. This is the God of the whirlwind, the flood, the plague of locusts, a God as impersonal as these forces of nature, a God who cannot be limited by human definitions or human morality.

Like any wise man confronted by some physically superior and unreasoning brute, Job capitulates. He propitiates God and eventually calms Him down. Finally God is satisfied that poor insignificant Job once more respects him sufficiently. At that he restores Job's health and wealth (though Job will have to have more children—those Satan killed remain dead, just as if they had no personal significance).

Yet, things will never be the same again for either God or man. By calling one part of God to judge another—even though he received no justice—Job has awakened a new thought into the godhead. By revealing his true nature to Job, God has also awakened to a view of himself that he had never tolerated before. Before Job, mankind's position vis-à-vis God was merely like the angels—to endlessly praise and obey. Now mankind has had the effrontery to judge God, to condemn God, to appeal to God's justice against God's injustice. God has been forced to reveal his multiple nature merely to quiet this disquieting little creature.

In short, we have revealed ourselves to be—at least in part—God's moral superior. God is forced to acknowledge that we (in our limitation but conscious unity) can see things that God himself (in His omniscience but unconscious multiplicity) cannot. It then becomes inevitable that God will be forced to accept limitation and definition and become human—in the person of Christ—in order to further develop. Once divinity descends into mankind, it is inevitable that our development will henceforth change God. Jung realized that modern humans are struggling with that polarity inside themselves—at once God and animal, trying helplessly to integrate these two seemingly incompatible sides just as Christ (and Buddha and others) did.

Without humans, God is static, unchanging in his essential nature. Only humanity can allow God to develop in his fullness. Modern humans struggle with a sense of purposeless because we can no longer accept any gods outside ourselves. We have withdrawn our projections from the outer world and found that "God is dead." But Jung reveals that—far from being dead—God is very much alive: inside us. Our great task is to transmute the godhead into its next incarnation, to serve as the cocoon that enables the butterfly to emerge.

In some way, this realization was already contained in *Seven Sermons to the Dead*, but Jung had not yet developed sufficient consciousness to see it. In some ways, the message was already contained in the original Gnostic heresy of Abraxas, but mankind wasn't yet conscious enough to see it. Only after a lifetime of dwelling in both our normal "consensus reality," and in the strange twilight world of the unconscious, was Jung able to see this strange truth. It remains to be seen how long it will take the rest of us to develop sufficient consciousness.

As we saw in the chapter 4, with the opening of the seventh seal, John's vision began a new cycle, a cycle which will attempt to deal with our attempt to reconcile the twin sides of our dual nature: the human as animal and the human as god. The first four angels cleared away the debris of the old world in their terrible fashion. Now with the fifth angel's trumpet ringing in our ears, we begin the history of that still-unresolved struggle between mind and body, a struggle that could only take place after Yahweh had given way to Christ, and Christ in turn had returned to heaven and yielded his place on earth to us.

CHAPTER 6

THE TIME OF TORMENT

And the fifth angel sounded, and I saw a star fall
from heaven unto earth: and to him was given the
key of the bottomless pit. And he opened the bottomless pit; and there arose a smoke out of the pit,
as the smoke of a great furnace; and the sun and
the air were darkened by reason of the smoke of
the pit. And there came out of the smoke locusts
upon the earth: and unto them was given power,
as the scorpions of the earth have power (9:1–3).

SEXUALITY VERSUS SPIRITUALITY

Sigmund Freud reawakened the Western world to the for-
bidden topic of sexuality. He reminded us that our instincts
can never be ignored; they are more ancient and more powerful than our barely adolescent logic and will. Jung vastly
extended Freud's work with his deeper understanding that
the instinctual drives, far from being ends in themselves,
are also indications of spiritual needs. The knowledge that
the highest and lowest are deeply entwined is a lesson
we—with our newly discovered rationality—overlook at
our peril.

> Freud's investigation of sexuality has made many
> valuable contributions to our problem. . . . Unfor-
> tunately Freud's very understandable over-valua-

tion of sexuality led him to reduce transformations of other specific psychic forces coordinated
with sexuality to sexuality pure and simple.[1]

At the molecular level, our body is a factory filled with
complex needs and complex solutions. The body finds the
raw materials it needs to manufacture the vast variety of
proteins, fats, carbohydrates, etc., necessary for continued
existence. That all proceeds totally isolated from our consciousness.

However, as we move up to the level of conscious
awareness of need, we only have a few primitive needs of
the body: the need for food and water, the need for sexual
release, the need for self-preservation. (Psychologist Abraham Maslow argued that when those primitive needs are
fulfilled, we then have a hierarchy of higher needs: status,
achievement, transcendence.) When we feel some inner
need for which we as yet have no category in our experience, we may feel it as a hunger—a literal hunger for food.
If we have developed into sexually mature adults, we are
likely to experience this unknown need not as hunger, but
as sexual need. This is especially true if the unknown has
burst through our defenses and has flooded us with energy.
Our only bodily experience of too much energy straining to
be released is sexuality. Therefore, we are likely to experience anything new and filled with energy as a sexual need.
We project it onto some possible new sexual partner as a
way of releasing the tension. Unfortunately, if the actual
need is not sexual, this does nothing more than temporarily
release tension. The new issue remains unresolved.

The mind-body struggle can never be successfully
resolved in favor of one or the other, for the two are inseparable. Rather, the struggle between body and spirit, if
accepted and lived through, brings the true human soul into

[1] C. G. Jung: *The Collected Works of C. G. Jung,* trans. R. F. C. Hull, Bollingen Series XX. Vol. 8: *The Structure and Dynamics of the Psyche* (Princeton,
NJ: Princeton University Press, 1960, 1969), ¶ 35.

existence. We seem to have a special place in existence, because we alone "consciously" mediate between the twin poles of mind and body. But then that will be much of the lesson that the Book of Revelation is trying to teach us, so I'll return to the fifth angel before I anticipate myself further.

FIFTH ANGEL SOUNDS HIS TRUMPET

With the sounding of the fifth angel's trumpet, a star plummets to the earth, breaks through the earth's surface and opens up a bottomless pit. Smoke bellows forth from the pit, darkening the sun and poisoning the air we breathe. From the smoke locusts come forth to torment those not fortunate enough to be marked as chosen by God. The torment is so great that *"in those days shall men seek death and shall not find it; and shall desire to die, and death shall flee from them"* (9:6).

> The moment of irruption [into consciousness] can, however, be very sudden, so that consciousness is instantaneously flooded with extremely strange and apparently quite unsuspected contents. That is how it looks to the laymen and even to the person concerned, but the experienced observer knows that psychological events are never sudden. In reality, the irruption has been preparing for many years, often for half a lifetime.[2]

It is with this "irruption into consciousness" that we have the true battleground of body and spirit that was presaged with the first four angels. First the star Wormwood fell into

---

[2] C. G. Jung: *The Collected Works of C. G. Jung*, trans. R. F. C. Hull, Bollingen Series XX. Vol. 7: *Two Essays on Analytical Psychology* (Princeton, NJ: Princeton University Press, 1953, 1966), ¶ 270.

the sea and poisoned it with its bitterness; then it is the earth itself that opens up: a "bottomless pit" that can never again be closed. The star comes from the sky, from the world of the spirit, seemingly far distant from the material worries of our daily lives. It breaks through the earth's surface to release the instinctual forces contained in the "bottomless pit" inside each of us.

THE "CHRIST" PROBLEM

When we are trapped between the pull of the spirit on one hand, and the body, on the other, we do feel that our sun is darkened and the very air we breathe seems poisoned. It is our unique state to be torn between those twin poles. This is the state of crucifixion that is represented for us by Christ. The unique vision of Christianity is that of a God-human, neither wholly one nor the other. If limited by self-definition to either god or human, the fullness of a Christ (or for that matter, a Buddha) cannot develop. It is just that almost intolerable struggle of seeming opposites that creates a Christ. Over sixty years ago, Jung discussed the role of the individual in bringing a new archetypal symbol (which in essence is what Christ and Buddha represent) into existence. His ideas are important enough to deserve the extended quotation which follows:

> . . . Only the passionate yearning of a highly developed mind, for which the traditional symbol is no longer the unified expression of the rational and the irrational, of the highest and the lowest, can create a new symbol.

> But precisely because the new symbol is born of man's highest spiritual aspirations and must at the

same time spring from the deepest roots of his being, it cannot be a one-sided product of the most highly differentiated mental functions but must derive equally from the lowest and most primitive levels of the psyche. For this collaboration of opposing states to be possible at all, they must first face one another in the fullest conscious opposition. This necessarily entails a violent disunion with oneself, to the point where thesis and antithesis negate one another, while the ego is forced to acknowledge its absolute participation in both.

If there is a subordination of one part, the symbol will be predominantly the product of the other part, and, to that extent, less a symbol than a symptom—a symptom of the suppressed antithesis. . . . But when there is full parity of the opposites, attested by the ego's absolute participation in both, this necessarily leads to a suspension of the will, for the will can no longer operate when every motive has an equally strong counter-motive. Since life cannot tolerate a standstill, a damming up of vital energy results, and this would lead to an insupportable condition did not the tension of opposites produce a new, uniting function that transcends them . . .

From the activity of the unconscious there now emerges a new content, constellated by thesis and antitheses in equal measure and standing in a compensatory relation to both. It thus forms the middle ground on which the opposites can be united.

. . . The stability of the ego and the superiority of the mediatory product to both thesis and antithesis are to my mind correlates, each conditioning the other . . .

> I have called this process in its totality the "tran-
> scendent function," "function" being here under-
> stood not as a basic function but as a complex
> function mode up of other functions, and "tran-
> scendent" not as denoting a metaphysical quality
> but merely the fact that this function facilitates a
> transition from one attitude to another.[3]

Thus Jung explained exactly how the individual could help bring a new symbol into existence. It requires the "passionate yearning of a highly developed mind" as well as the acceptance of a "violent disunion with oneself." To the extent that a person avoids the tension by giving primacy to either the spiritual or the instinctual side of the problem, the emerging product is "less a symbol than a symptom." If one bears the tension, and does not yield to the pull of one side or the other, "the tension of opposites produces a new, uniting function that transcends them."

Let's try to examine how this process might operate. Most of the time, traditional symbols are sufficient. For example, until very recently, the cross, as a symbol of Christianity, was sufficient as a container for our spiritual aspirations. But increasingly, with the development of science, religion has come to be regarded as irrelevant. Perhaps on Sundays we go to church and—for the space of a church service—allow ourselves to once more sink into the "container" of the Christian symbol. But when Monday comes, the "real world" impinges again, a world seemingly far from the childish values we listened to the previous day.

Now the real problem comes when we are confronted by a moral dilemma. All moral dilemmas have one foot in the material world, one in the transcendental. Only a living symbol can deal with such a tension of opposites. John's

---

[3] C. G. Jung: *The Collected Works of C. G. Jung*, trans. R. F. C. Hull, Bollingen Series XX. Vol. 6: *Psychological Types* (Princeton, NJ: Princeton University Press, 1971), ¶ 823–828.

vision is now telling us quite explicitly what these times—our times—are all about. Having passed beyond the world of mankind with the first four angels' trumpets, having seen that we can no longer ignore the "darkness" of the unconscious, we have come to the issue of our times, the issue foreshadowed throughout the entire Bible: the need for a resolution of the dichotomy between mankind as animal and mankind as god. On one hand, we can be an animal among other animals, connected to the land and the sea, the sun and the moon. Yet we can also be a god, feeling within ourselves—with a surety that passes beyond knowledge of the sensory world—the existence of something which transcends the earth and earthy concerns: something sublime, something holy.

The Book of Revelation is the last book of the New Testament. All the other books of the New Testament concern Christ's life and his mission on earth. The Book of Revelation moves forward to the end of time (i.e., it takes place in the metaworld of the collective unconscious which is beyond time). In John's own time, it wasn't yet possible to accept that we ourselves would have to bear the same burden as Christ. Our newly found Christ-consciousness (i.e., the knowledge of our essential divinity) had to be projected out onto Christ himself. But, unfortunately, that made it impossible to resolve the dilemma of the god/human because we couldn't acknowledge that it was our own dilemma.

> Christ the ideal took upon himself the sins of the world. But if the ideal is wholly outside then the sins of the individual are also outside, and consequently he is more of a fragment than ever.[4]

We have had nearly two millennia now to advance ever deeper into the center of the cyclone. We have progressed

---

[4] C. G. Jung: *The Collected Works of C. G. Jung,* trans. R. F. C. Hull, Bollingen Series XX. Vol. 12: *Psychology and Alchemy* (Princeton: NJ: Princeton University Press, 1953,1968), ¶ 9.

from the state of those early Christians, just beginning to grasp that humanity might have some connection with divinity; to the Renaissance, when we shouted out our new-born conviction that the measure of the universe was humanity itself; to the Victorians, convinced they were on the verge of bringing the universe to its knees.

During the 20th century, we have suffered almost a century of humiliation in every field of endeavor. Oh, we've had our triumphs: physical triumphs that dwarf the entire prior history of the species. But those triumphs have only brought more uncertainty, more despair. The 20th century has forced us to the humbling realization that our vaunted intellect is actually quite limited, while the universe we purport to dominate is infinite. We have had to unwillingly admit that we can never fit the godhead within our intellectual pretensions. It has been a long, bitter road we've traveled during this difficult century. Perhaps we are finally ready to hear the words of Revelation with the understanding that they speak to us as surely as they spoke to John.

THE PLAGUE OF SCORPION/LOCUSTS

> And it was commanded them that they should not hurt the grass of the earth, neither any green thing, neither any tree; but only those men which have not the seal of God on their foreheads. And to them it was given that they should not kill them, but that they should be tormented five months: and their torment was as the torment of a scorpion, when he striketh a man.(9:4–5)

The locusts that come from the pit have stingers like scorpions. They are the size and the temperament of horses bred for battle. Certainly a picture worthy of a modern horror-movie. Throughout the Bible, plagues of locusts personify the destructive wrath of the god of the Old Testament—Jehovah. Like fire and flood, they demonstrate the overwhelming, inhuman quality of nature unrestrained. Locusts didn't (and don't, since plagues of locusts are with us every bit as much as they were with our ancestors in the Bible) hurt people directly; they ate everything that grew, leaving parched land where crops had grown before. Their legacy was famine and slow death for human beings.

The people of the near-Eastern biblical region were equally familiar with scorpions, which abounded in the arid lands. Scorpions have an almost intolerably painful sting, but one that is rarely fatal. These scorpion-locusts were commanded not to harm grass and trees, but only people. Therefore, if you combine the inhumanly overwhelming quality of locusts with the burning, but not fatal, pain of the scorpion, you have an instrument which can inflict truly terrible suffering, a suffering not to be ended by quick death.

This is the suffering that we feel when the inhuman force of instinctual energy breaks through the thin crust of human culture. Remember that it was the spiritual force of the star from the heavens which broke through the earth, reminding us that spirit and instinct are forever entwined. John is describing the torment that many of us have already experienced, or will soon experience, a time when things have to become worse before they become better.

It was our desire for independence that led to the development of the god/human. We have already seen that the God Jehovah who confronted poor Job was stuck, he couldn't advance further without some new partnership with people. Yet, as we have also seen, a human being—as animal—just isn't capable of "containing" the godhead. Professed independence leads, in fact, to possession by the spiritual powers. God becomes demon. All because the spirit is beyond definition and when confined within the human, it swallows up the human. There is only one resolution: the creation of a new "living symbol." A true symbol is infinite, it can carry the spirit.

> God "is everywhere" and "not in the smallest place like the daemon." Thus one of God's attributes is infinity, whereas the distinguishing work of the daemon is limitation in space. Man as microcosm would then be included in the concept of the daemonic, and psychologically this would mean that the ego, separate and split off from God, is likely to become daemonic as soon as it accentuates its independence of God by its egocentricity.[5]

DESTROYING ANGELS

> And the sixth angel sounded, and I heard a voice from the four horns of the golden altar which is before God, Saying to the sixth angel which had the trumpet, Loose the four angels which are bound in the great river Euphrates (9:13–14).

The Euphrates is the largest river of western Asia, about 1, 700 miles in length. It joins with the Tigris river, one of the other great rivers of Asia. Most of the great cities of the ancient Mesopotamian civilization lay within the area bounded by the two rivers, including the greatest city of all—fabled Babylon, of which we'll hear more later. Most of us are more familiar with the great Egyptian cultures and their enormous dependence on the Nile. The Mesopotamian civilization was at least as dependent, if not more

---

[5] C. G. Jung: *The Collected Works of C. G. Jung*, trans. R. F. C. Hull, Bollingen Series XX. Vol. 13: *Alchemical Studies* (Princeton, NJ: Princeton University Press, 1967), ¶ 372n.

so, on the Euphrates. The Bible identifies both the Euphrates and Tigris as among the four rivers that had their source in Eden (the other two being the Pishon and the Gihon). Even today, despite the Leakeys' string of discoveries of early man and pre-man in Africa, it is still not unlikely that the original birthplace of man might have been the region between the Tigris and Euphrates rivers. However, whether or not it's our birthplace, it is a very, very ancient region.

In the vision, from this ancient region appear the four angels of destruction, just as the four horsemen of the Apocalypse appeared earlier in the vision. This is still another way of saying that the forces unleashed are instinctual forces from the deepest layers of the collective unconscious. When released by the fifth angel, the locust-scorpion-horses stung men with a pain so terrible they wished for death, but death wouldn't come. Now with the sounding of the sixth angel's trumpet, that wished-for death is finally at hand.

> By these three was the third part of men killed, by the fire, and by the smoke, and by the brimstone, which issued out of their mouths . . . . And the rest of the men which were not killed by these plagues yet repented not of the works of their hands, that they should not worship devils, and idols of gold, and silver, and brass, and stone, and of wood: which neither can see, nor hear, nor walk. Neither repented they of their murders, nor of their sorceries, nor of their fornication, nor of their thefts (9:18, 20, 21).

Once again, as with the first four angels, a "third" is destroyed, the vanishing middle. Yet even this is not enough to cause people to change their ways; they are stuck in definition, unable to change no matter how terrible the punishment. Haven't you ever experienced that state? The

Figure 9. When we blindly obey an external moral code, choices seem clear and easy. However, when we begin to follow our own inner path, decisions are no longer so simple, and it becomes much more difficult to separate good counsel from bad. ("Evil Counsellors," Gustave Doré, first published in *Divine Comedy*, 1868.)

answer is always around us, within us, waiting to be heard. But we stay stuck in our endless self-preoccupation, deaf to any new answer.

BOUNDARY CONDITIONS

All we really know of Earth is the tiny layer of land that lies on the surface where we walk and talk and live our lives. Just think about how big Earth is, and how small we humans are in comparison. The Earth is 8,000 miles across, while we are only five or six feet high. And even Earth, huge as it seems to us, is almost immeasurably small when we consider the universe, which is so much bigger that is no longer possible to measure on any human scale like feet or miles. In order to find a big enough measure for the universe, we have to use light-years; that is, the distance that light can travel in a year, moving at 186,000 miles per second. On that scale, Earth's diameter is one twenty-fifth of a light-second, the distance from Earth to the Sun is 8 light-minutes. Yet even the closest stars are over 4 light-years away.

So there we are, perched precariously on the edge of this planet which dwarfs us, and is itself not even a speck in the cosmos. It's at that tiny boundary between Earth and the heavens that life goes on.

Originally, in the unconscious, everything is in an undifferentiated unity. Consciousness comes about solely by creating opposition—hot and cold, hard and soft, good and bad, man and woman, etc. There is no quality that exists "in itself." If you're blindfolded and someone touches you with a piece of dry ice, you'll involuntarily snatch your hand away. The dry ice is so cold that you experience it as burning hot.

In the latter half of the 19th century, Ernst Heinrich Weber did a series of experiments attempting to discover the threshold of sensory awareness. He used objects of similar size and texture, but different weight. His subjects were blindfolded, then held one object in their hand for a minute. They then discarded the first object, held a second for a while and tried to decide which was heavier. Weber found that the heavier the objects, the greater the difference between the two weights had to be before the subjects could tell the difference. In other words, perhaps they could detect a difference of one ounce if the objects weighed about a pound. That same one ounce difference would be undetectable if the objects weighed closer to five pounds.

Weber didn't really appreciate what a great discovery he had made. A multi-faceted physicist/experimental psychologist named Gustav Fechner did. He codified it and generalized it into what he termed "Weber's Law": sensation varies with the natural logarithm of the stimulus. Fechner was excited because sensation was a purely mental process, while the stimulus was purely physical. Thus Weber's Law offered an example of scientific law which bridged the mind/body separation.

More broadly yet, we might consider Weber's Law as saying that all experience is relational. Let's bring that back to more human terms. If we can only define who we are in relationship to who we're not, then periodically we have to break down the existing boundaries, create a fluid condition for a while, then reestablish new boundaries (hopefully those boundaries move outward, so that our sense of who we are is enlarged). This doesn't happen easily because we are very reluctant to change our hard-won sense of self-definition. It takes a breakthrough—like the star Wormwood breaking through the earth's crust—to destroy the boundaries of the ego.

When the boundary is gone, the unconscious can pour forth, with its flood of undifferentiated energy. Our minds do their best to contain the energy even though our old boundaries have been destroyed. Much of the energy ends up labeled as sexual energy because that's just about the only thing most of us have ever experienced which has such overwhelming and inhuman power. Mystics and saints experience such a breakthrough in a different container—as a mystical or religious experience. In contrast, deeply disturbed people—whose egos are too fragile to withstand the flood from the unconscious—are overwhelmed and possessed by the collective material.

This chapter has been aptly named "the time of torment." Any breakthrough from the unconscious is frightening and painful to our ego consciousness. Until we discover spiritual "containers" for the unconscious material, we are pulled back and forth between opposites over which we have no control. The pain is so great that we will do almost anything to avoid it. Usually that means accepting one or the other side of the opposition between spirit and instinct presented to us by the unconscious. However, any such partial solution can only be temporary. When the issue is the conflict between the human being as animal and the human being as god, only a new definition of both will resolve the conflict.

Time after time in the vision, we see the war between the spiritual forces sent from heaven and the instinctual forces from below. We are continually torn between the two, able to triumph over neither. It is just that torment of indecision that has some hope of giving rise to the new. In the next chapter, we will explore the relationship between human beings and God in the hope of seeing some hint of a possible resolution.

CHAPTER 7

HUMANITY AND THE DIVINE

And I saw another mighty angel come down
from heaven, clothed with a cloud: and a rainbow
was upon his head, and his face was as it were
the sun, and his feet as pillars of fire, and he had
in his hand a little book open (10:1–2).

THE NATURE OF ANGELS

To make sure that we grasp the difference of the seventh—
in this case the seventh angel—once more the vision
shows the seventh as qualitatively different from the six
that preceded it. Imagine what an angel might be. As we
encounter them in the Bible, they seem both more and less
than human. They live by God's side and have powers far
beyond us. But they seem static in comparison with us.
The angels seem to be a set force, unchanging once
defined. Their tasks are to serve as intermediaries between
God and humanity, flying back and forth between heaven
and earth. They are present at great events, carrying out
God's tasks, or reporting the results back to God.

It is as if it were difficult for God to communicate
directly with us. And, indeed, when he does, it is largely
through some symbol that can safely contain his power,
like the burning bush before Moses, or the light that
appears before Saint Paul. We saw in the story of Job how
difficult it was for God to have a true communication with
us; seemingly the only way he could do so was to become
human in the person of Christ.

The implication seems to be that the distance between pure spirit and matter is too great to be bridged directly; intermediate symbols or vehicles like angels are needed. Therefore, when we encounter angels, they indicate some attempt to communicate between spirit and body, between God and human. Whether there are such things as angels is not really of importance to us, just as the literal truth of the entire vision is beside the point. We feel the need of something which mediates between ourselves and our conception of the sublime, and so such symbols exist.

Now the seventh angel is something special, even for angels, made up of nothing but heavenly materials: clouds, rainbow, sun, fire. In other words, he is built whole-cloth from spiritual material. It is very unlikely that a being that spiritual could even communicate with us; he's too far removed from matter. Therefore, if he is now appearing—and he does appear before John—it means that we are now very deep into the vision, far from material concerns. By the time we have reached the seventh angel of the seventh seal, we're spiraling ever closer to the world of the ineffable. But notice that the advance takes the form of a spiral of repeated cycles of seven rather than a straight line of linear progress.

> But in the days of the voice of the seventh angel, when he shall ban to sound, the mystery of God should be finished, as he hath declared to his servants the prophets (10:7).

SPIRITUAL MESSAGES AND PROPHESIES

> And the voice which I heard from heaven spake unto me again, and said, Go and take the little book which is open in the hand of the angel which standeth upon the sea and upon the earth. And I

went unto the angel, and said unto him, Give me
the little book. And he said unto me, Take it, and
eat it up; and it shall make thy belly bitter, but it
shall be in thy mouth sweet as honey (10:8–9).

John eats the book and finds it just as the angel described.
This heavenly creature has given John a little bit of spiritual
knowledge, just as much as he can swallow safely. Like all
experiences of the godhead, it is a wonderful thing at first,
but once it moves deeper inside, it becomes uncomfortable,
too big for us to contain. This creates the calling to prophesy,
the need to rid oneself of the burning message within. Matter
wasn't intended to carry the spirit lightly. Even Christ could
bear the full weight of both spirit and matter inextricably
merged, only with great personal suffering.

Therefore, for the much more human John (and so, too,
for you and me), even a "little book" of spiritual significance is bitter inside us, and has to be shared. The vision
doesn't say this, but experience of those who do share their
visions is that then the sweetness comes back to the taste.
As the heavenly message passes again over the lips, this
time outward, we taste once more the sweetness we experienced at first consumption.

I've mentioned the latter because it is one of the small
things we can do to ease our pain in this most painful of
transitions. Once we have been blessed—and afflicted—
with the knowledge that the world is not as we thought it to
be, there is a tendency to suffer the pain alone, curling up
with it like some suffering animal. But the animal in us
can't really ease the pain except by the momentary expedi-
ents of sleep or sex or any of the other "drugs" available to
our animal side. The pain comes from containing a spiritual
message too big for mankind alone. Therefore, we have to
behave as gods, prophesying and sharing our vision. At
such points, the god/man problem is resolved, because we
can function in both roles simultaneously. We are then solving the problem much as Christ himself did.

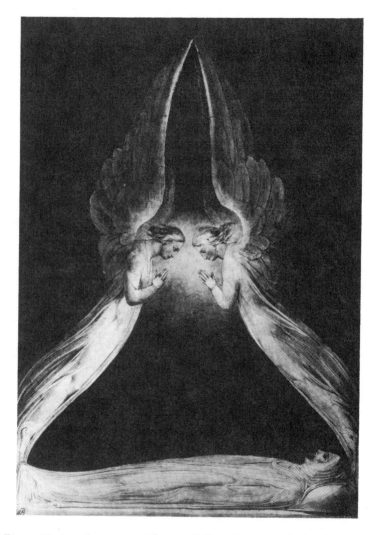

Figure 10. Angels represent the possibility of communication between
God and individual, between the spiritual and the material. In times of
transition, they serve as a bridge between the two. ("Angels watching
over the Tomb of Christ," c. 1806, William Blake.)

If that seems strange, think about the process. John is being given a new set of spiritual values to "swallow." Any such collective vision is too big for an individual; we can't contain it. Only a sufficiently big symbol, a symbol which can capture enormous numbers of people can contain new spiritual values. By prophesying, John is helping to bring a new symbol into existence. Now it's highly unlikely that any such symbol will be sufficient. Only when a great number of people bring forth strange new symbolic messages can they start to combine into a true symbol. But "swallowing" the spirit and bringing forth symbolic utterances is one path toward the future.

> . . . Their meaning [i.e., symbols] resides in the fact that they compensate an unadapted attitude of consciousness, an attitude that does not fulfil its purpose, and that they would enable it to do this if they were understood. But it becomes impossible to interpret their meaning if they are reduced to something else.[1]

It is always "safer" to keep our visions to ourselves. Whenever we go in a different direction from the majority of our fellow beings, we discover insights that we hesitate to share for fear of rejection. Let me tell the story of Hildegard of Bingen in the hope that it will convince the reader of the necessity for sharing our visions with the world.

HILDEGARD OF BINGEN

I have my home on high, I meet every creature of the world with grace.

---

[1] C. G. Jung: *The Collected Works of C. G. Jung,* trans. R. F. C. Hull, Bollingen Series XX. Vol. 13: *Alchemical Studies* (Princeton, NJ: Princeton University Press, 1967), ¶ 397.

God has arranged all things in the world in consideration of everything else.

The more one learns about that which one knows nothing of, the more one gains in wisdom. One has, therefore, through science, eyes with which it behooves us to pay attention.

Holy persons draw to themselves all that is earthly.[2]

Those statements were all written by a 12th century abbess, visionary, writer, painter, composer, scientist and social activist: Hildegard of Bingen. In discussing the source or her seemingly endless creativity, Hildegard wrote, "I had felt within myself the gift of secret mysteries and wondrous visions from the time I was a little girl." Like many others with similar experiences, she chose to keep those experiences largely hidden from others.

I revealed my gift to no one except a select few and some religious who were living in my area, and I concealed my gift continuously in quiet silence until God wished it to be manifest by God's own grace.[3]

The "religious" seemed to understand the strange little girl. Accordingly, when she was 8, her parents placed her in the care of a locally famed holy woman named Jutta. Sometime later, Jutta built a Benedictine abbey in the area, and it was there that Hildegard took the vows to become a nun. When Hildegard was 36, Jutta died and Hildegard was elected the

---

[2] Gabriele Uhlein, *Meditations with Hildegard of Bingen* (Santa Fe: Bear & Co., 1983), pp. 96, 65, 66, 64.
[3] Hildegard of Bingen, *Scivias*, translated by Bruce Hozeski (Santa Fe: Bear & Co., 1985), p. 2.

new abbess, a position she would hold until her death at
age 81.

But Hildegard found that something important was
still missing in her life. She wrote that she suffered from a
wide variety of illnesses—physical, emotional and spiritual.
Then, in Hildegard's words:

> In the year 1141 of the incarnation of Jesus Christ,
> the Word of God, when I was forty-two years and
> seven months old, a burning light coming from
> heaven poured into my mind. Like a flame which
> does not burn but rather kindles, it inflamed my
> heart and my breast, just as the sun warms some-
> thing with its rays.[4]

Still fearful, Hildegard concealed her vision for yet a while
longer. Finally, upon the pressure of several friends, she
began to write of her visions. As soon as she did that, her
health returned. Her first book, *Scivias* ("know the Ways")
was a record of her early visions, and an exegesis of the
meaning of her visions. Though *Scivias* took ten years to
complete, its fame grew as it developed. In 1147, the still
developing work was presented to the Pope, who was trav-
eling nearby. He openly admired Hildegard's great visions,
and asked her to continue her writing.

From that point until her death, Hildegard was famed
throughout Europe, both for the extraordinary character of
her written work, and *equally for her continued efforts to effect
change in the outer world.* Hers was a time when often the
quickest way to power and material success was through
joining the clergy (for a male, that is; there was no quick way
to power and material success for a woman). The "nobility"
of the church—its bishops and cardinals—were elected
largely from the nobility of the secular world for reasons

---

[4] *Scivias*, p. 2

Figure 11. Hildegard of Bingen was a 12th century abbess, visionary, writer, painter, composer, scientist, and social activist. As a young woman, she suffered from a wide variety of illnesses until she began painting the visions which welled up from within. Hildegard was that rarest of individuals, respected not only for her piety and creativity, but equally for her efforts to effect social change. (Hildegard of Bingen's fourth vision of the second part of *Scivias*, reprinted from *Hildegard of Bingen's Scivias* (Santa Fe: Bear & Co., 1986), p. 100. Used by kind permission.

more material than spiritual. Hildegard was openly critical of anyone, including kings and popes, who allowed their spiritual mission to become confused with material gains.

However, Hildegard was also a practical woman who realized that spiritual aims have to be effected in a secular world. In contrast to many lesser mystics, then and now, who scorn the outer world as an inferior mirror of the inner world of their visions, Hildegard celebrated the physical world she lived in. Hildegard's sickness had come from remaining an introverted recluse, from her refusal to share her visions for fear that they would be rejected. Her health came from overcoming her fears and opening herself to the world in a uniquely feminine way.

HALF-LIVES AND ZENO'S PARADOXES

Each time in the vision, when we reach the mysterious "seventh," the vision always has some sort of pause to make sure that we grasp that one cycle had ended and another is about to begin. Since we're deeper in the vision, this pause is now more dramatic. Having become a prophet with the consumption of the "little book," John is now about to be given the real vision that he will prophesy about.

> And there was given me a reed like unto a rod: and the angel stood, saying, Rise, and measure the temple of God, and the altar, and them that worship therein. But the court which is without the temple leave out, and measure it not; for it is given unto the Gentiles: and the holy city shall they tread under foot forty and two months (11:1–2).

First, he is given a measuring rod with which to measure the temple and altar and "them that worship therein." But not the court outside where the "Gentiles" will have a free reign for a period of forty-two months; i.e., three-and-a-half years, half of seven years. That is, John is now to get the measure of God's dwelling and the sort of person who can live within God's precepts. The point is that the new is coming, and the old ways won't work anymore. John is to get his first taste of the new.

Just as we have the seemingly endless chain of cycles of seven (more will follow), an interesting variation is now beginning: a half-cycle of three-and-a-half, sometimes expressed directly, sometimes as forty-two months, sometimes even as twelve-hundred-and-sixty days. It is reminiscent of the half-life of radioactive elements. There half is destroyed in a given length of time, then half of what remains in the same length of time, and on and on. The process is endless; though the amount remaining grows smaller than any amount you might pick, it never entirely disappears.

Or consider Zeno's paradoxes in their many forms. They all boil down to the fact that you can't view something as both finite and yet infinitely divisible at the same time. If the tortoise is given a head start on the hare in the famous race, the hare can never catch up, Zeno argues. By the time, the hare arrives at the place where the tortoise began, the tortoise—though ever so slowly—has moved beyond. By the time the hare arrives at this new location, again the tortoise has moved further. The hare can get closer and closer, but never catch the tortoise.

That's what the three-and-a-half, half of a "seven" cycle, reminds us of, in John's vision. It is as if, as long as we remain immersed in the world of the half-life, the empty world of shadows which is all we know, it will seem to go on forever, half-life after half-life after half-life. But if we step outside of this gray rut, we see that it indeed comes to an end, and in a finite amount of time, just as in reality the hare would pass the tortoise in a finite amount of time. This vision is not of time as we know it.

THE TWO WITNESSES

> And I will give power unto my two witnesses, and
> they shall prophesy a thousand two hundred and
> threescore days, clothed in sackcloth. These are the
> two olive trees, and the two candlesticks standing
> before the God of the earth. . . . These have power
> to shut heaven, that it rain not in the days of their
> prophecy: and have power over waters to turn
> them to blood, and to smite the earth with all
> plagues, as often as they will (11:3, 4, 6).

The first such half-cycle has begun; the Gentiles, the non-believers, rule the courtyards for three-and-a-half years. Two "Witnesses" are sent to prophesy to mankind during those forty-two months. They are "two olive trees," "two candlesticks." In other words, in this "half-cycle," "two" is the significant factor. Consider the nature of "two." When there is only "one," everything is undifferentiated; there is no-thing, so "one" and "nothing" are identical.

As we discussed in the previous chapter, it is only when some distinction is made between things, only when a boundary separates into "two," do we have the development of individuality. When "twos" begin appearing in dreams—twins, for example—it marks a time just before something is ready to emerge into consciousness. The new birth from the unconscious is trying to find an identity acceptable by consciousness, but is not quite able to yet.

Also consider the concept of a "witness." A witness observes an event, then testifies to what has been observed. "Witness" comes from the Old English word "wit," meaning "knowledge." So a witness has knowledge that can be communicated. God's two Witnesses are witnesses in two different ways: (1) they are on earth to observe humanity's actions and report them to God; and (2) coming from heaven, they can report God's words to humanity. They can go in either direction, much like the angels God sends to communicate with man. The Witnesses mark a stage when the spirit is one step closer to conscious realization.

The Witnesses possess fearsome powers: they can kill with fire, stop the rain, turn waters to blood, send plagues. Clearly, if we stay stuck in this half-cycle by refusing to hear the voice from the unconscious, the half-cycles will go on endlessly. The Witnesses' express purpose is to force us to see the new vision that God is sending, to turn us toward the spiritual message. But, like all the other forms of messenger that God has already sent, the Witnesses are fated to be unsuccessful in bringing people to an acceptance of God's new world. It's still too early in the vision—more turns around the spiral are still necessary.

> And when they shall have finished their testimony, the beast that ascendeth out of the bottomless pit shall make war against them, and shall overcome them, and kill them. . . . And after three days and a half the spirit of life from God entered into them, and they stood upon their feet; and great fear fell upon them which saw them. And they heard a great voice from heaven saying unto them, Come up hither. And they ascended up to heaven in a cloud; and their enemies beheld them (11:7, 11, 12).

Thus the oscillation continues: something from the spirit, something from the earth, Witnesses from heaven followed by the beast from the pit. You'll recall from the previous chapter that the pit was originally created when the star Wormwood fell from heaven; i.e., when the spiritual forces were so strong that they broke through our resistance and released compensatory instinctual forces. Spirit and instinct—two sides of the same coin—have to war within us until some new reconciliation is found. Unfortunately, since we are not willing to hear the spiritual message the Witnesses bring, we are destined to be dragged down by the beast of instinct.

After three-and-a-half days (another half-cycle!), the Witnesses rise from the dead and ascend into heaven just like Christ before them. Christ ascended to heaven because it wasn't yet time for all people to accept their condition as both God and human. Similarly the Witnesses ascend to heaven because we are still not ready to hear that message. An earthquake follows and it is finally time for the seventh angel to sound his trumpet.

> And the seventh angel sounded; and there were great voices in heaven, saying, The kingdoms of this world are become the kingdoms of our Lord, and of his Christ; and he shall reign for ever and ever (11:15).

This chapter has been leading gradually up to a new consideration of the theme we began in chapter 4: the evolving relationship between humanity and God. We've examined the nature of angels as a bridge between God and human, the pain of containing spiritual messages which leads to the need to prophesy, the "half-lives" of seeming endlessness which can trap us if we don't learn to step outside them, the nature of "witnesses" who mark a stage just before conscious realization. Now it's time to examine Jung's concept of the Self: the bridge between man and God which we contain within ourselves.

SPIRITUAL UNDERPINNINGS OF NEUROSIS

> If the supreme value (Christ) and the supreme negation (sin) are outside, then the soul is void; its highest and lowest are missing.[5]

---

[5] C. G. Jung: *The Collected Works of C. G. Jung*, trans. R. F. C. Hull, Bollingen Series XX. Vol. 12: *Psychology and Alchemy* (Princeton, NJ: Princeton University Press, 1953, 1968), ¶ 9.

It was Jung's experience that when an analysis continued long enough and delved deeply enough, it eventually hit spiritual depths. In fact, he felt that all psychological disturbances in the second half of life were (in some part) spiritual crises. Jung's conclusion isn't really so shocking when carefully considered. Mental illness, unless organic, is always a reflection of emotional disturbance. The patient (who is most probably you or me in these unusual days) is depressed, or alienated, or confused, or isolated—all emotional issues. Underneath emotional conflicts lie conflicts of morality, of values, and that's where our spirituality lives.

Most of us aren't accustomed to thinking about psychological problems as having anything to do with spiritual values. We can talk glibly of neurosis and psychosis, of id and ego, of complexes and even archetypes (for those who are as knowledgeable about Jungian psychology as Freudian). It's easy to forget that Freudian psychology began with an attempt to deal realistically with the basic facts of human experience, with simple core issues common to all of us. As animals, we have natural urges to eat when we are hungry, defecate when we feel an inner pressure to eliminate excess waste, have sex when we feel tension created by an excess of energy, etc. But we are taught that we can only satisfy those needs under conditions allowable by our parents (initially), then later by other authorities (teachers, ministers, scout leaders, coaches, etc.), still later by society itself in all its personified forms, and eventually only if those needs satisfy some abstract moral code that we carry inside us.

These psychic prohibitions create an inner conflict between the needs of society and the needs of our body. Because of that conflict, our body generates emotions that have no acceptable outlet. We conceal not only the initial urge—the lust, the hunger—but also the emotion generated within us by the conflict between the unfulfilled urge and the prohibition of morality: our anger, sadness, frustration.

We turn those emotions inward upon ourselves. When the emotion needs to come out badly enough, we get mental illness as an attempt to resolve the impasse.

In a depth analysis, these conflicts emerge a little bit at a time, and hopefully are resolved. A patient discovers that his parents need no longer dominate his life; as an adult he can choose actions that satisfy his needs despite the fact that his parents punished him for those same actions as a child. He learns to develop a broadened morality that better fits his adult personality.

But there are many levels to the human psyche. After resolving the conflicts with parents and other external authority figures, much still remains; in fact, *most* still remains. Jung found that, stripped of the personal experiences which we all accumulate over the course of our development, there are deeper impersonal levels to the psyche. These levels are aspects of the collective unconscious.

JUNG'S CONCEPT OF THE SELF

> Even if it were only the relationship of a drop of water to the sea, that sea would not exist but for the multitude of drops. [Speaking of the relationship of the individual soul to God].[6]

For our purposes at this point, we are most interested in the central organizing aspect of the Collective Unconscious, a personified function that Jung termed the Self (capitalized to distinguish it from the normal use of the term self). Virtually all mystical traditions (the covert, esoteric religious traditions rather than the overt, exoteric religion which most of us learned while growing up) teach that God is found

---

[6] Carl Jung, *Collected Works*, Vol. XII, ¶ 11.

not in some distant heaven, but within our individual souls. Esoteric religion aims at producing a inner union of our personal identity with those transpersonal parts of our psyche that transcend earthly experience.

> The Eastern attitude (more particularly the Indian) is the other way around; everything, highest and lowest, is in the (transcendental) subject. Accordingly, the significance of the Atman, the Self, is heightened beyond all bounds. [In the West] the notion that there can be psychic factors which correspond to the divine figures is regarded as a devaluation of the latter.[7]

Jung independently discovered the existence of a "transcendent function" within the human psyche. This function transcends not only our conscious desires and needs, but also the primitive desires Freud characterized as coming from the *id*. This function continually serves to both center our lives and evolve us toward some seemingly pre-determined goal. Since this function normally was personified in dreams, visions, myths, fairy tales, etc., as a godlike older figure (though it takes many, many other forms, both anthropomorphic and abstract), Jung termed it the Self, to denote a wiser figure within who—though godlike—was still part of our total identity.

In chapter 4, we discussed Jung's *Answer to Job*, in which Jung had the audacity to claim that Job was God's moral superior, and that henceforth God would take on human form. It's time now to pull back slightly from that audacious claim. Jung was quite clear that the Self was not God; rather, the Self was all that a human could experience of God. The Self is like a funnel through which the infinite transcendence of God can be reduced to a form which, while transcending anything we can ever experience in the

---

[7] *Collected Works*, Vol. XII, ¶ 9.

world of our bodies, is still capable of human experience. Thus the story of Job is a story of the relationship between our normal human consciousness and the Self, at a critical point in the history of consciousness.

Jung's concept of the Self is not an attempt to reduce religious concepts to psychological terms. Quite the contrary, Jung is instead insisting that there are unexpectedly vast aspects to the human personality, aspects that provide some possibility of bridging the seemingly unbridgeable gap between God and human being. Through the Self, each of us can deal directly with God, just as surely as Moses or Abraham or Job did. Further, if the experience of the Self changes as we develop, and changes in all mankind, as mankind develops, it marks how our capacity to deal with God is changing. That was the real point of Jung's *Answer to Job*.

WHY THE VISION STILL SPEAKS TO US

> . . . An image can be considered archetypal when it can be shown to exist in the records of human history, in identical form and with the same meaning. . . . In consequence of the collective nature of the image, it is often impossible to establish its full range of meaning from the associative material of a single individual.[8]

As humans, we can't really think about anything for which we have no mental concept, no symbol; without symbols there is no such thing as thinking. What we can't symbolize, we can't express in either words or behavior. Correspond-

---

[8] C. G. Jung: *The Collected Works of C. G. Jung*, trans. R. F. C. Hull, Bollingen Series XX. Vol. 13: *Alchemical Studies* (Princeton, NJ: Princeton University Press, 1967), ¶ 352f.

ingly, all the verbal and behavioral expressions mirror our inner symbols. Because of this mirroring of inner and outer, it's possible to look at the outer expressions of any culture— its rituals, its religion, its art, etc.—and understand what mental concepts were available to people in that culture. The outer aspects of the culture reflect the inner; our creations mark what we were capable of thinking at any point in history.

That is one reason why this book is being written. Certain themes emerge over and over, in our times, in our lives. The Book of Revelation was written at a time when a new stage of consciousness was developing: the stage of the integration of God and human, as expressed in the personal lives of Christ and the Buddha. When this new stage of consciousness first began, only a few could experience the god/human within themselves. Most had to project it outward onto a Christ or a Buddha. Early Christians read the Book of Revelation as a symbolic expression of outer events.

If the Book of Revelation holds our interest today, it is because it once more expresses the state of our collective psyches at a momentous point in history: the point where the integration of God and human becomes general, not confined to a chosen few. Eighteen hundred years after its composition, we are finally at a stage of psychic development where we can look at the events pictured in the vision, not as pictures of external events, but as symbols of internal problems and of possible solutions to those problems. We can see the vision as a dream so great that it captures the hearts and souls of all of us at the same time.

THE SENSE OF THE SACRED

Therefore, when we speak of God in John's vision, let us consider Him for now as the Self, this mighty transcendent being or force within each of us. Let us see Christ as a certain stage of experiencing that force: the stage where body and spirit are indestructibly commingled. The vision says that "the Kingdoms of this world are become the kingdoms of our Lord." That is, the Self, our experience of the sacred, pervades everything. In the early stages of a depth therapy, there comes a magical moment when a patient first realizes that everything that happens in his or her life has a psychological underpinning. This is such a powerful discovery that he or she feels like Archimedes did when he said that if he could have a long enough lever and a place to put the fulcrum, he could move the earth. Just so, the patient feels that he or she has a way to get outside the individual problem and "move" it through the impersonal force of psychological understanding.

Collectively, mankind first reached that same stage of insight with the dawn of the Renaissance. Suddenly, we realized that we could stand outside nature and observe it. Rather than being merely a part of nature, subject to its whims, we could subsume the multiplicity of nature within our minds. In our minds, we could discover orders inherent in nature, or create new orders undreamed of by nature. Once conceived, more thought could bring actualization. Observation led to power.

But there are more depths than that to both nature and the psyche. Even though the patient solves emotional problems, a need still remains: the need for meaning. Though collectively mankind has used intellect to achieve physical mastery over the world, the same need still remains: the need for meaning. When the vision says that "the Kingdoms of this world are become the kingdoms of our Lord," it signifies more than just an intellectual subduing of nature. In the vision, this is the time of judgment of the dead, the time when the temple of God is opened in heaven. In other words, now the transcendental realm is open to our personal experience. We might now expect that this spiritual world will open itself to our vision one piece at a time.

CHAPTER 8

THE SNAKE IN THE GARDEN AND OTHER CREATION MYTHS

Man becomes aware of the sacred because it manifests itself, shows itself, as something wholly different from the profane. To designate *the act of manifestation* of the sacred, we have proposed the term *hierophany*. It is a fitting term, because it does not imply anything further; it expresses no more than is implicit in its etymological content; *ie., that something sacred shows itself to us* . . .

. . . It is impossible to overemphasize the paradox represented by every hierophany, even the most elementary. By manifesting the sacred, any object becomes *something else,* yet it continues to remain *itself,* for it continues to participate in its surrounding cosmic milieu. . . . In other words, for those who have a religious experience all nature is capable of revealing itself as cosmic sacrality. The cosmos in its entirety can became a hierophany. [Eliade's emphasis in all cases above.][1]

THE SACRED AND PROFANE

The relationship between consciousness and the unconscious is deep and mysterious. When we let consciousness loose, we are able to participate directly in the unconscious.

---

[1] Mircea Eliade, *The Sacred and the Profane*, (New York & London: Harvest, 1959), pp. 11f.

Figure 12. In many creation myths, including those from the Egyptians and the Jews, a serpent figures heavily in a drama marking a transition from an unconscious stage to the beginnings of consciousness. Because life is always more difficult after such a change, the serpent has been unfairly presented in a negative light. ("The Serpent," Gustave Doré, first published in *La Sainte Bible,* 1860.)

We drive cars, tie our shoes, play tennis, with little or no conscious awareness of our actions. In a deep trance or deep meditation, we are able to participate in the collective unconscious itself. But when we try and bring our consciousness to bear, the unity with the unconscious disappears. When we try and find some boundary condition where we can meet the unconscious with our consciousness, symbols invariably appear.

Thus Moses experiences God as a burning bush, Jonah experiences God's inhuman might as a whale which swallows him, etc. We can only consciously perceive the sacred in the dress of some symbol of the depths, some archetypal image. Whenever possible, the unconscious seems to prefer to personify psychic elements, because we deal most easily with other people like ourselves. Thus, modern Christians present God to their children through the portrait of the "little baby Jesus, asleep in the hay." Buddhists personify God through the simplified story of the events which led Prince Siddhartha Gautama to his enlightenment.

Whether God is wearing the trappings of "little baby Jesus" or Prince Gautama, it is still God who is being presented. Or rather, it is the Self, which is as much of the sacred as humans are capable of experiencing. In dealing with the sacred figures from the unconscious, we must be careful not to confuse the actor with his role, for an actor can wear many robes and play many roles in his life. Jung made an attempt to discriminate between the multiplicity of figures we encounter in our dreams and the archetypes that underlay that multiplicity.

THE CELESTIAL WOMAN
AND THE GREAT DRAGON

And there appeared a great wonder in heaven; a woman clothed with the sun, and the moon

> under her feet, and upon her head a crown of twelve stars: and she being with child cried, travailing in birth and pained to be delivered.
>
> And there appeared another wonder in heaven; and behold a great red dragon, having seven heads and ten horns, and seven crowns upon his heads (12:1–3).

Biblical times were an overwhelmingly masculine era. The Jewish religion which bred Christianity is a religion with almost no contact with the feminine. Therefore, the fact that a feminine symbol is encountered in the depths of the unconscious is an understandable compensation for the overemphasis on the masculine in the conscious outer world. Given the predominantly masculine character of that epoch, it seems likely that the spiritual might have been encountered as feminine even by the women of the times. But, in any case, the needed complement in our Vision is the feminine archetype. This feminine figure, who has taken so many forms in so many times and cultures, is seen here as the mother of the coming era, as Mary is the mother of Christ (and hence the Christian era) and Isis of Horus (of which more will be said later). This celestial woman—in both John's era and our own—is in pain waiting to deliver her child. (We will have a good deal more to say about the missing feminine in later chapters.)

All this is straightforward and understandable. If the unconscious wants to show us that our old days are at an end, what better way than by the series of cycles we have seen already in the vision: e.g., a book that can only be opened by one who has died; a book with seven seals, and opening each of them is accompanied by disasters and omens that take us farther away from the world we know; the seventh seal yielding seven angels, each releasing further disasters that bring our known world to an end. If the psyche—at this seeming end point—wants to stress that this is not only an end, but also a new beginning, what better way than to show a celestial woman "clothed with the sun, and the moon under her feet," pregnant and experiencing the pains of labor.

The old never yields gracefully to the new, there is always resistance and struggle. In this case, that resistance appears in the guise of a great red dragon with seven heads and ten horns. But even this beast is royal: it bears seven crowns on its seven heads. This is the apotheosis of our dying era, with its seven upon seven: this is Satan!

Everything bad begins with a good idea; everything good, if taken too far, degenerates into something bad. This seven-headed dragon started out quite small, as the small green snake that tempted Adam and Eve in the Garden of Eden. If we are to know what to make of this great beast, we have to once more leave our vision and talk of the Garden of Eden.

THE FIRST CREATION STORY OF GENESIS

In the beginning God created the heaven and the earth. And the earth was without form, and void; and darkness was upon the face of the deep. And the Spirit of God moved upon the face of the waters. And God said, let there be light: and there was light. And God saw the light, that it was good: and God divided the light from the darkness. And God called the light Day, and the darkness he called Night. And the evening and the morning were the first day (Genesis 1:1–5).

. . . the first day of creation begins with self-knowledge. . . . by which is meant a knowledge not of the ego, but of the Self, that objective phenomenon of which the ego is the subject.[2]

---

[2] Carl Jung, *Collected Works*, Vol. 13, ¶ 301.

Figure 13. The creation of Adam marks the first emergence of a differentiated consciousness. Adam's first task is to name the animals, something God is seemingly not himself capable of doing. ("God creating Adam from a lump of clay", Illustration from William Caxton's Bible, late 15th century.)

Jung had a deep interest in creation myths; he felt that they symbolized the birth of consciousness in the depths of the unconscious. We'll discuss the biblical creation myth in that light. Similarly, Mircea Eliade felt that all strivings for first principles are a search for a time beyond time, a yearning for a world beyond history: in other words, a search for the sacred. Such mythologies appear to be the most primitive of all religious expressions.

The Bible juxtaposes two separate creation myths within the Book of Genesis. The first is the story of the creation of the world out of the formless chaos. This story begins with the words "let there be light," and proceeds to the creation of humans and animals on the sixth day. In this first creation myth, each thing in itself, each unique entity, is allocated one day of creation: light and darkness; earth and water; plants; time (for that is what the fixed lights in the heavens were); birds and fish, the creature of the depths and the heavens; and finally the animals, including humans. After the six days of creation, there was a day of rest—the seventh day. By this time, I'm sure that it is abundantly clear that the seven indicates that we are going to cycle through the material again at another level.

This first great creation is impersonal; it is similar to a scientific theory or a mathematical proof. There is no human element in it; humans are reduced to just one more item in the list of created things (though God does give human beings dominion over all the animals). I'm surprised that, in the periodic debate between scientists and creationists, it isn't realized that the Bible itself recognizes that there is a place for the impersonal, scientific side, a side that doesn't involve humans and their emotional attachments. And what a stirring place the Bible accords it: at the very beginning and blessed with some of the most glorious language of the entire Bible. Every scientist knows the exultation that lies in the impersonal contemplation of the cosmos, freed from humanity's troubles and doubts.

In this first great explanation of creation, the Bible presents a very great concept: that the world evolved across time, and that there are certain totally disparate things within that evolution: light (or energy), earth and water, plants, animals, time. About the only thing we would add currently is that we believe that all the animals evolved from common ancestors, rather than the birds and fishes differing from the land animals, as the Bible states. But still it's a remarkably accurate scientific presentation of creation. However, the Bible is not intended to be merely a book of scientific facts. Having expressed a complex scientific view of creation in a beautifully concise manner, the Bible passes to its true subject: human beings and our relationship with the godhead.

MONOTHEISM AND THE ORIGINS OF RELIGION

And the LORD God formed man of the dust of the ground, and breathed into his nostrils the breath of life; and man became a living soul. And the LORD God planted a garden eastward in Eden; and there he put the man whom he had formed. And out of the ground made the LORD God to grow every tree that is pleasant to the sight, and good for food; the tree of life also in the midst of the garden, and the tree of knowledge of good and evil (Genesis 2:7–9).

Having finished one cycle of seven with the seventh day of rest, the Bible proceeds to another cycle through the same material. The second great creation story tells of Adam and Eve and their expulsion from the Garden of Eden. In the first creation myth, creation was described in impersonal, scientific terms (though filled with gorgeous poetry). In this second myth, things are much different: everything is presented in relation to mankind. The problem of the god/human, which would later find concrete realization in the person of Christ, is explicitly presented at the very beginning of creation. The Bible tells that God made Adam "of the dust of the ground, and breathed into his nostrils the breath of life; and man became a living soul."

Thus humans are both matter ("the dust of the ground") and spirit ("the breath of life"); it is that unique combination which gives us a soul. From that moment of creation, humans were destined to follow the crooked path we have traveled for so long now: from the desire to eat the fruit of the Tree of Knowledge; to Joseph's ability to understand dreams; to Job's torment by God and Satan; to the birth of the god/human: Christ; to our own seemingly insoluble dilemma. For we are not just creatures of the "dust of the ground," no different from any other animal. We are also composed of spirit, of the breath of God. With that first infusion of the spirit, that tasted so sweet at first, just like the little book that John ate, something would grow bitter inside us and demand that we give voice to our need, our longing. From the moment of creation, we could never be satisfied with a wholly animal existence.

As Genesis shows us, this feeling of oneness with divinity is not a recent, sophisticated religious expression. Rather, it appears to be the most primary of all experiences of the sacred. Historians of religion have long discarded the once accepted idea of humans progressing from a primitive animism, to a slightly more sophisticated polytheism, to the culmination of a monotheism (like you and I believe in, sophisticated creatures that we are). No, the first religious experience seems much more likely to have been a belief that there is a single principle that is holy, and that we have a direct connection to the godhead. Of course, to talk of first anythings is almost impossible. As Eliade tells us in almost the same breath, this yearning to find a first principle is itself a primitive expression of that same first religious belief. So, like the endless cycles we have seen in the vision, the need to find first principles in religion is itself a first principle in religion.

Humans are created as both animal and God. In this second creation myth, the point is driven home. Only after Adam is created, are the plants of his world, the waters of his world, the minerals of his world, and the animals of his world, created. And the animals are only fully created when Adam names them.

NAMING THE ANIMALS

This is a great moment in the story! By naming the animals, we demonstrate that they are concepts contained within us. And the man who names them is named himself: Adam. The Bible does not make an issue of God naming Adam, though it does make an issue of how he was created. It merely mentions in passing that after God had formed all the birds and animals, he brought them before "Adam to see what he would call them."

So, clearly, Adam as a concept is so contained within God that he doesn't even make a point of deciding what to name him; he just *is* Adam. But God does not know what Adam will name the animals—he waits to see what names Adam will give them. "And whatsoever Adam called every living creature, that was the name thereof." It appears that humans are intended by God to be the center of the world, the measuring rod by which everything will be judged. (That is why it is so significant in the vision that John was given a measuring rod with which to measure the temple of God, but we will have to ignore that, for the exploration of this great vision can indeed be endless.)

Isn't the whole issue raised by Jung in *Answer to Job* already implicit here? If God does not know what the animals will be named until Adam names them, then we can see that humanity can serve a key purpose for God. Jung struggled with this issue continuously over the last years of his life: what was the purpose of consciousness? He knew that the collective unconscious seemed to contain all knowledge within itself, yet he had recognized in his own life that he had to develop his own values, not automatically accede to the values presented to him by the unconscious. While the unconscious was beyond time and place, while it had access to unlimited knowledge and power, it was diffuse. Human consciousness, like some specialized scientific tool, could explore the fine points of existence.

Thus, in this second great creation story, in the first book of the Bible, the western world's most sacred book, Jung's heresy is presented: from the beginning we can do things for God which God can not do directly for himself!

TREE OF KNOWLEDGE

God puts a restriction on Adam: he must not eat the fruit of the "tree of knowledge of good and evil." If Adam eats the fruit, God tells him that he will die. But there is a puzzle inherent in the story already. If man can't recognize good and evil, how is he to rule over the earth and the animals thereon? If he has no moral choice, how is he to going to deal with the spirit with which God has infused him? What is this soul God has made uniquely for man, if man has no self-recognition? In other words, it appears that man, by his very nature, his unique combination of mind and body, is destined to eat the fruit of the tree.

The Bible presents it as a matter of pride. Adam and Eve eat the fruit because they want to be like gods. But what else can they desire to be? They have been given the spirit of God as well as the body of an animal. However, I would suggest

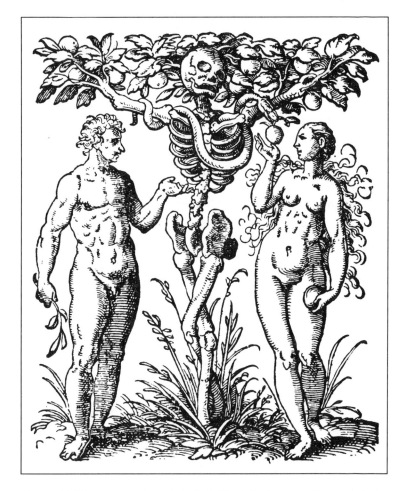

Figure 14. The unconscious state feels like bliss because it is entirely in the moment, with no memories of the past, or fears of the future. In contrast, consciousness is continually confronted by the possibilities of an unknown future leading ultimately to death. ("Macabre representation of the Tree of Knowledge and Death, a woodcut by Jost Amman, from Jacob Rueff's *De conceptu et generatione hominis,* Peter Fabricus, Frankfurt, 1587.)

there is something to be learned from treating it as a choice of pride. Anyone who has ever made any spiritual advance in life knows how easy it is to assume that he or she has become a very wonderful person, almost a god. It is almost a given in therapy that you need to balance the extremes of a client. When the client has little feeling of self-worth, the therapist quite rightly points out what a marvelous, unique person the patient really is. But when the patient becomes inflated with too high a self-evaluation, the therapist, again rightly, attempts to deflate the patient, to point out that there is a long way to go toward divinity or even full humanity.

We just can't handle this god-substance, this spirit, we contain within ourselves. If we decide that we are spirit, it possesses us and we fill up with false pride. If we try to deny the spirit within and limit ourselves to our animal nature, we feel sad and empty, bereft of all purpose. Our story seems to be the story of an attempt to answer the seemingly unanswerable: how to merge god and animal into one being?

In Genesis, the serpent is introduced as a creature "more subtle than any beast of the field." That implies that the serpent must also possess knowledge of good and evil. He must be something different than either the animals or man. Interestingly, the serpent serves this function in other myths. One that bears closely on the Bible's story is the Egyptian myth of why Ra revealed his name to Isis. Let's look at this myth before we move on with the evolution of the spirit, since it tells us a great deal about the nature of that evolution.

RA AND ISIS

In the Egyptian myth, Ra was the supreme God, the God who created all things. But he had grown old and senile and doddered slowly around, spittle falling from his lips.

Figure 15. In Egyptian creation myths, Ra was the first differentiated supreme god. Eventually he grew old and ill. This marked the time when a transition was needed to a new stage of consciousness. ("Amen-Ra, King of the Gods, Lord of Heaven," reprinted from *The Gods of the Egyptians*.)

Isis carefully formed a snake out of the earth and put it on the ground where Ra would pass by. When he did, his spittle fell on the snake and gave it life. Once alive, the snake bit Ra, causing Ra great pain.

Ra was perplexed: nothing existed except that which he had created and he had not created anything which could have done this to him. So he had no idea how to cure himself. Meanwhile, he grew sicker and sicker. He called Isis to his side to see if she could help him, because he had made her a great healer, among her other attributes.

Isis said that she could do nothing unless she knew Ra's secret name. This is another way of saying that she would possess his power. The ability to name something means that one is conscious of all that the named thing is; naming is a conscious realization of some archetype of the unconscious. That is why it is so important that the Bible says that Adam names the animals and even God is not aware of their names until Adam names them.

Ra tries to evade the issue by giving many of his names, names that are merely descriptions of functions, not the true name. This would correspond to mere intellectual knowledge, for intelligence can only define something in terms of what it is made up of, or appears like, or functions as, or . . . in other words, only in terms of material nature, not spiritual nature.

Finally, Ra gives in and tells Isis his true name. Possessing it, she is able to cure Ra, but he has lost his power in the process. With this passage of power, the age of Ra gives way to the age of Osiris, Isis' husband (of whom we'll hear more later in this book). We find of interest the fact that the snake is here, as in Genesis, the intermediary when some of the supreme god's power is passed on. In the story of Ra and Isis, it is quite clear that this is a necessary step. Ra is presented as old and tired. The problem seems to lie in the fact that creation is limited to Ra; none of his creations can themselves create.

Figure 16. Isis formed a snake from the earth and lay it in Ra's path. When Ra's spittle fell on it, the snake came alive and bit Ra. He grew ill, but Isis refused to heal him until he told her his secret name. With that name came his power, which Isis passed on to her husband, Osiris, who became the new supreme god. This was the beginning of ego consciousness. ("The Goddess Isis," reprinted from *The Gods of the Egyptians*.)

The ability to create, knowledge of one's identity, awareness of good and evil, are all bound together. Just as the Bible recognized that Adam can name the animals, undoubtedly because he is partially one of them, the story of Ra and Isis recognizes that true knowledge of the creator enables one to create. Both stories talk of a necessary step in the development of consciousness.

The serpent is a needed component is this drama, one who is unfairly condemned as evil. However, there is one sense in which he is evil and we need to understand that, just as much as we have to understand that he serves God's purpose. If God creates Adam in order to do the things which God himself cannot do, then God has to present Adam with both sides of the issue. At the same time that God breathes his own spirit into Adam, he also has to convince Adam of their utter separation. He says in effect: "I am spirit, you are body. So long as you do not aspire to be spirit, too, you will remain happy" (i.e., unaware). But God also has to awaken man to his spiritual nature; until man is aware of that, there can be no conflict and, therefore, no possibility of growth. How can both be accomplished?

In the story of Ra, we have some hints. As I have already said, no one but Ra could create. The world was static, unchanging. What was needed was evolution! And evolution implies that there is continual creation. Every change in nature is a little creation. This is a point of great interest and even greater complexity. Let us merely assume it for now, since trying to explain it at greater length would consume much of what this book hopes to address later. Let's just accept that the stage marked by the passage from Ra to Osiris (or from Jehovah to Christ) is the stage of passage from a static world to an evolving world.

To express that in terms of the psyche, this is the stage where the eternal archetypes pass into consciousness, where they can develop and change.

THE EVOLUTION OF SPIRIT

Hence, this is a necessary passage, but one which is seen as threatening by the old static God—by Ra or Jehovah. Every parent experiences this same dilemma with their own children. At one and the same time, they want their children to both fulfil their own unfulfilled dreams (i.e., the dreams of the parents) and yet to be their own person with their own dreams. That's an irresolvable conflict, because the child has to have independence in order to develop, but that very independence estranges parent and child. God wanted mankind to evolve and change; the world could not remain unchanging any longer. But God hoped that this could be done painlessly; that wasn't to be.

Until he eats the fruit of the Tree of Knowledge, Adam is not a true mixture of matter and mind, body and spirit; rather he is matter imprisoned by spirit, matter with no control over its own destiny. The spirit tempts to the other extreme: spirit imprisoned and controlled by matter. The temptation to be one with the Gods is more than that; it is really the temptation to be greater than the Gods. For the Gods are all spirit and humans are both matter and spirit. That is the evil preached by the serpent; that is why he will always be reviled.

It would be nice if life did not have to be so hard, if Adam and Eve could continue to dwell in Paradise, slowly evolving into the new being for which God hoped: neither wholly man nor God. But that's not the way of the world. In our own times, we are experiencing the issue in the attempts of women to gain masculine power and assertion, men's attempts to gain feminine relatedness and rootedness. Anyone who has ever watched someone go through the process knows that the men initially become maudlin and dependent, the women pushy and rigid. Development comes from swinging to the opposite extreme, then back again to the old, on and on in a pendulum swing which gradually damps, gradually finds a resting place in the middle. So, too, is mankind's own development.

Once upon a time, there was nothing but spirit, one with itself and unchanging. Then somehow (for this is perhaps the greatest mystery), it became aware of itself. It examined itself and noticed facets of itself. These facets thus attained a separate existence as well as remaining part of the whole. This is the stage where Ra created the other Gods. This is where the archetypes come into existence. They are fluid and amorphous—at their edges, one archetype flows into one another. Trying to pin any archetype down in definition ineluctably leads one to still other archetypes in an endless procession.

When the spirit accepts more limitation, more definition, it forms matter. This is interesting to spirit because it is different than spirit, yet is part of spirit since it was created from spirit. But it is still unchanging. The world is static. Once spirit has examined all of itself, identified each of its attributes, once it has created something separate from itself, but unchanging also, there is no further place for development.

Only when spirit limits itself further, allows itself to be held within the confines of form, in an uneasy tension between the two, can continuous, evolutionary change take place. That is why mankind was created.

I'm afraid that all these topics are infinite—like the archetypes themselves—and each leads to other topics. But I must at least point out here Teilhard de Chardin's concept that consciousness resides in everything: more in humans, less in animals, less still in plants, down and down endlessly, to quarks and beyond. Unless something of that sort were true, there could be no evolution. But in this chapter, I am talking of a more particular form of consciousness: the full recognition of self that we think of as identity.

We have had to take a long detour through Genesis, and the Egyptian creation myth of Ra, in order to find out what the purpose is for the serpent, and why it is regarded

Figure 17. Before Horus, before Isis and Osiris, even before Ra, were the primordial waters of chaos, of Nun. ("The Creation," reprinted from *The Gods of the Egyptians*.)

as evil. Before we finally return to the Book of Revelation and John's vision, let us just note a few more details about the serpent in this light.

First, it is Eve that is first tempted by the serpent, and who in turn tempts Adam. The Bible is telling us specifically that this pull toward the Godhead comes from our feminine side, from those things we regard as feminine. That is: our emotions, sentiments, moods, intuitions, all convince us that we are not just animals like other animals. It is through emotions that we experience something of the spirit, some union with God which allows us to know that we are more than biological creatures. That is a very important teaching. Of course, the Jewish Old Testament is a product of a patriarchal culture, so the issue is presented from a masculine point of view. In a feminist Bible, it would be man who was created from woman—as every man from that time to this has been—and man who tempted woman. A woman experiences spirit through her thoughts, her abstractions, her ability to impart definition and meaning to reality. There she experiences that oneness with God which drives her to be more than just an animal among other animals.

Second, because the serpent tempted Eve, God tells him: "I will put enmity between thee and the woman, and between thy seed and her seed; it shall bruise thy head, and thou shalt bruise his heel." Therefore, our pride will always be at war with our emotional depths, our hopes to reach the stars always bruised under the heel of physical limitation. Mankind will always have an Achilles Heel, a weak point where we touch the earth; we can never stand firmly enough on the earth to have a place to launch ourselves toward the heavens.

Finally, the serpent continues to exert the same role throughout the Bible, present at each new stage of evolution. Each time we gain some new ability to merge body and spirit, there is the serpent of overweening pride to suggest that this time we are ready to be more than God. From the Garden of Eden to the temptation of Christ on the mountain, the role of the serpent (or Satan) is the same.

Therefore, when we see the great dragon in John's vision, we have little reason to believe that he preaches anything new. We now know something more of the Dragon—a serpent grown great. We know of its role as midwife to consciousness, of its overweening pride, and of its special relationship to the feminine. By this final transitional stage in human development, the lowly serpent has grown into the mighty Dragon. The birth at which it presides is the greatest in mankind's history, for after millenniums of development, our consciousness has reached an impasse. Unable to solve any of the seemingly insoluble problems confronting it, much of our life energy has become confined, forced into the unconscious. The time of gestation is nearly complete and the unconscious is ready to give birth to a new level of consciousness. However, pride has grown to comparably gigantic size, ready to swallow this new birth as soon as it is out of the womb.

We have reached a critical time in the evolution of consciousness. This new consciousness must be carefully guarded and protected against our arrogance.

CHAPTER 9

MIGHTY BABYLON HAS FALLEN

. . . the dragon stood before the woman which was ready to be delivered, for to devour her child as soon as it was born. And she brought forth a man child, who was to rule all nations with a rod of iron: and her child was caught up unto God, and to his throne. And the woman fled into the wilderness, where she hath a place prepared of God, that they should feed her there a thousand two hundred and threescore days (12:4–6).

A FALSE DEPRESSION

Here then, the new life—male because it is written from a masculine perspective—finally comes forth. But it has to be spiritualized first; i.e., when the new is finally born in us, we have to let the psyche contain and protect it for a while. At such times, our emotional connection with life leaves us; we feel not tormented as we did when the child was still to be born, but without emotion.

All of us have experienced such moments in our life. After a long period of gestation—of struggle and moral pain—we give birth to something new inside us. There is a brief moment of exultation at the release of pressure, and a brief glimpse of the beauty of the new. Then a flatness of affect sets in; we feel virtually nothing. Nature abhors a vacuum; at such times, it is very easy for a mood of depression to envelop us because of the absence of emotion. It behooves us to try and avoid this "false depression." Gestation requires a true depression: a withdrawal of energy into the unconscious; such a depression should be honored. But this brief period of emotional absence can be over in an eyeblink if we don't become confused and drift into depression.

> And there was war in heaven: Michael and his angels fought against the dragon; and the dragon fought and his angels, And prevailed not; neither was their place found any more in heaven. And the great dragon was cast out, that old serpent, called the Devil, and Satan, which deceiveth the whole world: he was cast out into the earth, and his angels were cast out with him (12:7–9).

This is a clear presentation of the dragon as Lucifer, the greatest of the angels, who dared to challenge God. But why is the battle taking place now? Hasn't that battle taken place long ago? This is a vision beyond time; in the world of the psyche; events happen over and over again. In a small way, the new Christ is born many times in each of our lives, the avenging angels come over and over again to tear down the obsolete worlds we construct. And Satan is thrown down from heaven many times.

More specifically, this happens at this point in John's vision because, with the new life already safely in heaven, there is no longer a place in heaven for a Satanic element. As long as there was yet no new life, the pride within us could still hope to rule body and spirit. Once the new life is born and taken into our spirit, there is no more hope of the flesh subduing the spirit. All that is left at this moment is the flesh itself.

> And when the dragon saw that he was cast unto the earth, he persecuted the woman which brought forth the man child. And to the woman were given two wings of a great eagle, that she might fly into the wilderness, into her place,

> where she is nourished for a time, and times, and half a time, from the face of the serpent.
>
> And the serpent cast out of his mouth water as a flood after the woman, that he might cause her to be carried away of the flood. And the earth helped the woman, and the earth opened her mouth, and swallowed up the flood which the dragon cast out of his mouth (12:13–16).

So—having been thrown from heaven—the Serpent tries to catch the woman, but is continually thwarted. First he pursues her and she flies away. Then he vomits a huge torrent of water to drown her and the earth swallows it up. Thus, in desolation at being unable to prevent the new from being born, our old pride tries to possess our emotions. But by this time we have—through the long struggle of emotional gestation—made our peace with our emotions; they are now firmly rooted in the earth of our physical life. They can no longer be so easily drowned as they once might have been. However, we are also not yet capable of understanding our new situation.

A CRISIS OF FAITH

> And I stood upon the sand of the sea, and saw a beast rise up out of the sea, having seven heads and ten horns, and upon his horns ten crowns, and upon his heads the name of blasphemy.
>
> And the beast which I saw was like unto a leopard, and his feet were as the feet of a bear, and his mouth as the mouth of a lion: and the dragon gave him his power, and his seat, and great authority (13:1–2).

Cut off from heaven, unable to destroy the new birth, the Dragon is left to run rough-shod over the earth, doing what he wills. This is the time of the Anti-Christ. In John's vision, a "beast rises up out of the sea" who blasphemes against God. He overcomes the saints and acquires power over the people of the entire world, who fall down and worship him. Then a second beast comes from the earth and serves the first beast in the same way that John the Baptist served Christ—prophesying for him.

Try to imagine this time within the microcosm of your own experience, then try to extend it to the macrocosm of the collective experience of our troubled time. In our individual lives, we have all experienced a moral crisis, where our old values were no longer adequate to the complexity of the situation before us. These crises of faith are usually preceded by a period of sterility, a period when we no longer experience any joy in our life. At such a time, life offers no possibilities. Not only do we feel depressed, we are convinced that we will always feel depressed.

When the gray veil of depression slowly begins to lift, it is because we become aware of some new interest in life which we are able to invest with energy, drawing it out of our unconscious. However, this new interest is virtually always in conflict with our old values. We find ourselves caught in a dilemma, because our old values tell us that the new thing is wrong, yet we feel attracted to it. This is always a bitter struggle. If we merely accept the new thing wholeheartedly—ignoring our values—nothing is settled. Without struggle, we merely experience the new toy briefly, then grow bored with it again.

What we have to do is struggle between the fixed and comfortable values of the old and the fluid and frightening values of the new. What has to emerge is something different, a new birth. When that time of struggle—which can be very long indeed—finally ends and the new life is born, like all new life, it is fragile and vulnerable at first. Thankfully, we usually find that it is protected for us during the period when we can't protect it ourselves. Is there anyone who hasn't felt that their major life changes were directed by some force larger than themselves?

Just as a mother is exhausted after a long delivery, we stand bereft of emotional connection, without strength to battle anymore. This is a time when the old tries to make one last stab at controlling us. Our old values, so much a part of us that they know every twist and turn of our needs and wants, change shape. They present their old messages in new ways; they offer us the external riches of the new life without any of its responsibilities. This is the time when faith is needed. Something in us knows that the new has already been born, that it is right and should rule, and that we must wait for it to take its rightful place. We must resist the blandishments of the Dragon and his tool—the Beast.

Fortunately, this is normally a short period of time, nothing like the period of sterility, even less like the period of gestation. This is just a mere cough punctuating a prayer, but even in this brief time, one can fall from grace and lose all that has gone before.

CHUTES AND LADDERS

Anyone who has ever played the ancient game of "Chutes and Ladders" (or "Snakes and Ladders" in some versions) knows about this. Players progress steadily around and up a board, depending on the throw of the dice. If they are lucky, they may land on a square showing the bottom rung of a ladder. They can then pass immediately up the ladder to a higher level. But they can also land on a chute (i.e., slide) and slide down, sometimes back to the very beginning of the game.

"Chutes and Ladders" developed out of an Indian oracular device called "Leela." A player's movement along the board marked progressive stages of conscious development. The "ladders" or "swords" symbolized the swift gain we can experience due to a special insight; the "chutes" or "snakes" symbolized vices that led to spiritual downfall. In our own times, the same theme has been repeated in endless video games—like "Donkey Kong"—where players try to steadily advance to progressively higher levels, but are always in danger of falling back to where he started.

This is a period in the vision where it is possible to fall down a "chute," or be bitten by a "snake," and lose everything. Though this is a slight challenge compared to those which have gone before, it can still be dangerous.

THE BIRTH OF A NEW SYMBOL

Now imagine that this event is happening not in our individual lives, but in the wider world. Imagine how much deeper the struggle, how much more energy is involved, how much greater the birth needs to be. Over sixty years ago, Jung discussed the role of the individual in bringing a new archetypal symbol into existence. Jung said this about the birth of a new "living symbol" (as he called a major change in consciousness):

> . . . Since, for a given epoch [a living symbol] is the best possible expression for what is still unknown, it must be the product of the most complex and differentiated minds of that age. But in order to have such an Act at all, it must embrace what is common to a large group of men. This can never be what is most differentiated, the highest attainable, for only a very few attain to that or understand it. The common factor must be something that is still so primitive that its ubiquity cannot be doubted.[1]

When John wrote his vision, the new symbol that was trying to be born was the symbol of the god/human. We have dis-

---

[1] C. G. Jung: *The Collected Works of C. G. Jung*, trans. R. F. C. Hull, Bollingen Series XX. Vol. 6: *Psychological Types* (Princeton, NJ: Princeton University Press, 1971), ¶ 820.

cussed this already at some length, but there is much more to say about it. If the series of events, which I have followed in the Book of Revelation, captures our dreams and fantasies, if the psychic states it symbolizes are going on inside enormous numbers of us at the same point in time, then we are discussing a change in Consciousness itself, not just a change in our individual consciousness. Think of that. Why did the birth, life, and death of Buddha, of Christ, of Mohammed, capture the minds and souls of large portions of the world community? They could only do so if the event was taking place in something much bigger than individual men and women. The Germans speak of a "Zeitgeist," a "Spirit of the Times." Such a "Zeitgeist" is sweeping our times. I am suggesting that it is the major event of at least the last two thousand years, perhaps of the entire history of mankind.

As we have already discussed, the Bible can be viewed as the history of the development of consciousness, as portrayed through the changing relationship between God and mankind. The Bible takes us from the birth of consciousness in the Book of Genesis, through the changes in consciousness represented by the stories of Abraham, Isaac, Jacob, Joseph, Moses, Job, David, etc.; each has a different relationship with God, each a different stage in the development of consciousness. All lead up to the birth of Christ: the true God/human, fully spirit and fully body.

But John's great vision takes place after all this, even after Christ has once more ascended into heaven, which should be the ostensible culmination of the Bible. I'm suggesting that even the great event of Christ's life was only a major episode in a larger story. We are only now approaching the real finale: the birth of a new stage of consciousness, which bears the same relationship to life as we know it, as Christ does to Adam. Adam contained Christ from the moment when God created him, but what a long struggle to pass through the unbroken line which led from one to the other. Imagine a world where Christ is the new Adam, as far away from the next apotheotic figure as primitive mankind with the first glimmerings of self-awareness is from the god/human that we know as Christ.

So let us not dwell long on the brief, lamentable period where the Anti-Christ rules, putting his mark on those of us too tired and sore to keep the vision of the newly born Christ before our mind's eye. Let us pass quickly to the Scarlet Woman, to Armageddon, the Millennium and the Last Judgment, and past these to the reason for the vision— the New Jerusalem!

In a way, everything has now been written and the time is prepared for the New Jerusalem, the new world of consciousness that is ready to begin. But again I stress that the world of the vision is timeless, and we see the same event from many different perspectives, each carrying some part of the truth, each trying to activate that part of our souls that knows the whole truth, that only needs to be awakened. Think of works like *Absalom, Absalom* and *The Sound and the Fury* by Faulkner. The message in all is not merely that the same event is experienced differently by different people. The deeper understanding is that, within the world of sensory experience—the world where all of us live when cut off from the spirit—there is no final truth. This is why the Book of Revelation approaches the same inner events over and over, from so many viewpoints. This vision has eternal symbols for its alphabet, any one of which could reveal the whole if properly experienced. And so, though we have already heard all that we need in order to know what is passing away and what is to come, we have yet to experience it through the filter of some of the Bible's most powerful images.

THE SCARLET WOMAN

So he carried me away in the spirit into the wilderness: and I saw a woman sit upon a scarlet coloured beast, full of names of blasphemy, hav-

ing seven heads and ten horns. And the woman
was arrayed in purple and scarlet colour, and
decked with gold and precious stones and pearls,
having a golden cup in her hand full of abominations and filthiness of her fornication: And upon
her forehead was a name written, MYSTERY,
BABYLON THE GREAT, THE MOTHER OF
HARLOTS AND ABOMINATIONS OF THE
EARTH. And I saw the woman drunken with the
blood of the saints, and with the blood of the martyrs of Jesus: and when I saw her, I wondered
with great admiration (17:3–6).

The world is a wonderful, dazzling, enticing creature, a
beautiful woman who has kept us entranced from the first
temptation to eat the fruit of the Tree of Knowledge to these
final moments, when her finery seems a little shabby and
her charm a little strained. This beautiful woman is our next
image, but first the vision gives us another cycle of seven,
summing up the whole affair, and still another cycle following that. But both are brief since the end approaches.

Soon after the appearance of the Beast and his false
prophet—the second beast—come seven angels to sing the
song of the end. They announce that the hour of Judgment
has come, that Babylon is fallen, that God's anger is upon
us, that the earth is about to be consumed by fire and
plagues. Following hard on their heels are seven more
angels, ready to visit plagues upon the earth. Again, as so
many times before in the vision, they deal with the world as
we know it in four stages, then beyond the known world in
the final three stages. Then, again as before, we have the
entire world, referred to here as Babylon, split into thirds.
Hail falls from heaven and we have had a quick preview of
what is to come.

But what of Babylon, this beautiful creature we once
worshiped as Mother earth, who has only become a whore
because we have made her one? That is the next great

Figure 18. Just as man experiences "Woman" through women, he experiences both the world and the spirit through these images of women. This is the archetype Jung called *anima*, which represents the possibility of relationship with someone or something other than oneself. ("The Goddess Heresy" from a satiric anti-Reformation handbill designed by Anton Eisen, Paderborn, Germany, late 16th century.)

symbol to confront. Here she is described as a "great whore that sitteth upon many waters," as a "woman sitting upon a scarlet colored beast . . . arrayed in purple and scarlet color." On her forehead are the words: "Mystery, Babylon the Great, Mother of Harlots and Abominations of the Earth." She is "drunken with the blood of saints, and with the blood of the martyrs of Jesus." And yet, after all that atrocity, when John sees her, he says that "I wondered with great admiration." She is clearly a formidable woman.

Men and women experience gender through the men and women in our life, and the succession of roles they play. First, for both boys and girls, there is the mother who bears us and nourishes us. It is initially difficult for a baby to realize that "mother" is a separate being. But soon that discrimination occurs, and children start to separate things into categories. The first such category is undoubtedly the relationship with the mother, and soon afterward, the father and siblings. Gender identification begins very early, with boys imitating fathers, girls their mothers, each making sharp distinctions between men and women largely on the basis of that experience of their parents. As they play with brothers and sisters, then with other children outside their family, they begin to try out these newly identified gender distinctions. It soon becomes much more comfortable to play with children of the same sex. That makes them specialize in the characteristics of their given gender role.

However, despite this strong gender identification, mother remains special. All children, whether boys or girls, remain dependent on their mother. As they slowly gain a sense of identity, including gender identity, they are able to do so only because they can always turn back to the support of the mother. Of course, things would undoubtedly be different if humans were one of the animal species where children are raised by the male parent. However, even in our species, children identify their relationship with the opposite sex parent as something different. Girls, like boys, may turn to the mother in time of need, but it's the father with whom they have a special relationship. Boys may feel this draw to the mother in even larger measure, because the concepts of mother and woman are so intertwined for them.

In adolescence, men and women experience each other as lovers. Here, for the first time, they feel something that can compete with their mother and father for their attention. Young men and women delight in the experience of a lover delighting in the experience of them. They are astounded at their wonderful individuality, overcome with the realization that they are the one and only person on earth who can capture this lover. This is intoxicating and new, because all children know somewhere inside themselves that the love of their parents is indiscriminate: they would love any child, as long as it was theirs. That is confining, limiting. In contrast, this new love has chosen them from among many others. Nevertheless, there is a great sense of loss at sacrificing the security of childhood; only the strong pull of sex and love can overcome that sense of ennui that is so characteristic of adolescence.

Still later, men and women experience each other as mates, as the mother or father of their children. Here they realize that, by sacrificing some of their newly-won individuality, they can attain immortality. They give up part of themselves to the mate, and gain a child, a new creation that partakes of both and which will live after both are dead. Again, as when they left parents for lovers, there is a sense of loss, but a greater gain. When they left their parents, they gained a unique identity at the expense of a loss of security. When they leave their lovers for their mates, they lose some of their identity, but gain immortality.

The experience of mother and father, brother and sister, friend, lover and mate is such an essential part of our lives, that we can hardly avoid experiencing the world through the same images. The world can be our parent, hopefully nourishing and comforting, guiding and protecting us like a good parent, but perhaps leaving us hungry and unloved, without support or direction, like a bad parent. Then we can know the world like our siblings and childhood companions: as other than ourselves, but still someone we can share life with, that we can compete with and enjoy. That experience yields to the world as loved one, as someone so enticing that we can't believe our luck. That passes as well, and we find that the world is the mate through which we can create something new that will live after us.

This is what Jung meant by archetypes. The anima and animus are especially strong archetypes because men and women have experienced the opposite sex in some variety of the same roles throughout our entire evolutionary development. Inevitably we have transferred that experience onto many other things in the twin worlds of matter and spirit. That experience shared by so many for so long gathers energy about itself, until something is formed that transcends individuals.

Some would argue that nothing is created, that there is no such thing as an archetype, that people merely experience the same things because the world changes very little ("the more things change, the more they stay the same" as the saying goes). This argument is logically sound, almost unarguable. However, that isn't the way the world seems to work, no matter how much we would like to reduce the spirit to mere matter (or behavior as we term it in our not very enlightened age). Experience convinces us otherwise, regardless of logical arguments to the contrary. For we experience the archetype first, and the world through the filter of the archetype!

IMPRINTING AN ARCHETYPE

There is a lovely picture from naturalist/ethologist Konrad Lorenz' book *King Solomon's Ring* that perfectly captures this for me: Lorenz is strolling along, followed by a baby duck waddling behind in the way baby ducks have always waddled behind their mothers.[2] Lorenz was present when this orphaned duck hatched, and the baby duck "imprinted" the archetype of mother on Lorenz. Somehow, the little duck already knew what mothers are for, and turned to its strange mother—Lorenz—for food and love. It also tried to learn the ways of the world from mother, hence the picture of the duck waddling in Lorenz's wake.

Now clearly this duck didn't need to have the world teach it what a mother was: it already knew. And equally clearly this idea of a mother wasn't some inner picture of a mother duck, because Lorenz didn't look much like a duck. The little duck must have contained a concept of mother that awaited concrete form in its actual mother. Or, since mother wasn't available, in Konrad Lorenz.

Like the little duck, we contain archetypes of Mother and Father, Sister and Brother, Friend, Lover and Mate, each filled with aeons of experience of these roles, each awaiting the opportunity to take concrete form in our own lives. Just as important as it is to realize that these forms are eternal and eternally experienced in our lives, is the realization that each of us experiences them in a unique form in our individual lives. No one else experiences the Mother archetype through the form of your particular mother in your particular circumstances. The archetype is eternal and so slowly changing that it almost seems unchanging. But the individual experience of the archetype is almost infinitely different.

When the eternal world of spirit takes concrete form in the world of matter, then individuality comes into existence. Only humans can name the world and its experiences because only humans consciously combine spirit and matter. We can begin to see just how important our

---

[2] Konrad Lorenz, *King Solomon's Ring* (New York: Crowell, 1982).

role is. As time passes, and we experience the people and things of the world over and over, slowly changing our perception, the archetypes begin to reflect that change. This is a slow, slow process because there is always a larger and larger accumulation of past experience that our new, individual experience has to balance against, but still they change.

If it were only that, we might be justified in the view that the Serpent constantly tempts us with—the belief that we are greater than the gods. But it isn't only our experience that slowly, inevitably changes the spirit. When the time of change comes, first comes the spirit, then the material manifestation. The new is experienced first through those exceptional ones who are closest to the spirit: the Christs, the Buddhas. Only afterward does the spirit descend slowly into the rest of us where it slowly evolves into something new, that can then in its turn pass back again into the world of spirit—the collective unconscious. The spirit is always the directing force, the creative force, but we also have our role. Only through individual experience of the spirit can we give its particular manifestation a name, a definition. That act of creation by naming, while smaller than God's creation, is also truly creation, and a very heady wine to experience.

THE GREAT WHORE

What then does it mean that the world—Babylon—is now seen as a Great Whore, a Scarlet Woman? Where is the nourishing Mother Earth? Where the sister, the lover, the mate? We seem to have gone wrong somewhere.

A prostitute is a woman who sells her body to a man, a woman who offers sex for a fee. This way, sex can be reduced to a purely physical action, with no necessary emotional attachment. By paying a material bill, a male avoids any more valuable payment. How does such a thing happen? If sex were just a natural physical act for us, as it is for other animals, there would be no such thing as a prostitute. But sex is not merely a physical act. In the Garden, the first thing Adam and Eve experienced after they had eaten the apple was an awareness of sexuality, a sense of shame at their nudity. Clearly, sex means more to us than it does to an animal.

Our oldest taboo is the prohibition against incest. Books have been filled with discussions of the reasons for such a prohibition. It formed the cornerstone of Freudian theory. But to look at it very briefly from the point of view I'm considering here, doesn't the incest taboo have a clear purpose? It prevents the roles of Mother and Lover from mixing. If the male awareness of feminine is the main vehicle through which he views the "other," whether the "other" is a woman or the world or the spirit, then males have to develop all the necessary and separate views of woman. They have to advance through the evolving archetypes of woman as Mother, Sister, Lover, Mate.

Once the male has experienced them all, he learns to discriminate between them. He can separate the nourishing love of a mother from sisterly love, from the passionate love of a lover or the tender love of a mate. He can view women in one or the other of these roles as the need arises. He can even view women as combinations of these roles, not because the roles are so fuzzy for him that he can't separate them, but rather because they are so clear and well-defined that he can distinguish fine subtleties among the roles. And, of course, if he can do this with women, he then has separated off the inner experiences of women, the different faces of the Anima archetype, and is free to experience the world and the spirit through the same archetypal windows. He is a well-rounded personality.

If there were no prohibition against incest, then that separation and discrimination would never occur. Males would stay in the grip of a mother's nourishing, but also paralyzing, love. So the incest taboo is necessary if men are to grow. But, given that, we ask again: why does a prostitute's role evolve? It has the effect of separating sex and love. Sex can be provided by the prostitute for money as the physical need arises, with no necessity for any emotional relationship, now or later. Thus the incest taboo is defeated in its purpose. A male doesn't have to leave his mother to obtain sex; he can pay for the sex and stay with mother for her undifferentiated love. And so, of course, the male's view of women doesn't fully evolve, doesn't develop the further archetype of woman as lover. Separated from the physical depths of sexuality, a lover is merely another form of mother.

Many psychologists these days speak of this problem as the Madonna/Prostitute Complex. In brief, the concept is that a male afflicted by the Madonna/Prostitute Complex can only see a woman as good or bad: good if she is idealized and unattainable, bad if she is physically attainable. Such a male may marry, but his real sexual interests are in prostitutes or a series of short-term affairs with women he perceives as "bad" and, hence, desirable.

We could follow the evolving roles of women throughout history and understand the evolution of consciousness, much as our study of the Book of Revelation has led us to do with the relationship between God and humanity in the Bible. For example, it's difficult to find a time so ancient that mankind was not able to separate the archetypes of sexual lover and mate. Yet a further separation of the two archetypes began with the inception of the "courtly love" tradition in the 12th century. We are still struggling with that separation today, though we have come a long way in developing an inner, emotional answer to the problem.

But, at the time of writing the Book of Revelation, that wasn't yet an issue. The males of that era were able to see Woman as their personal mother, and Woman as the mother of their children, but Woman as sexual lover was still seen as Eve, tempting them to a world of struggle and strife. A

Figure 19. Just as the evolution of consciousness can be traced through the changing relationship between god and mankind, it can also be traced in the changing relationship between men and women. As that relationship has become more complex, the number of roles available for women has slowly evolved and developed over time. It is currently at a critical moment of transition. (Top: "Chambermaid and matron;" bottom: "Bride and prostitute," from *La dance Macabre des Femmes*, Antoine Verard, Paris, 1486.)

sexual woman could only be an evil woman—the Great Whore!

The Great Whore's name is Babylon, the greatest city of the ancient world. In the first to second century, A.D., when the Book of Revelation was written, Babylon's greatest days were fully six to seven centuries in the past; for the past four to five centuries, the city had been of no significance in the world. At this point in history, the great city of the world was Rome, and so most interpreters of the Book of Revelation interpret this part of the vision as talking of Rome's upcoming fall,

But we don't need to be constrained by that interpretation. We can imagine Babylon as it still was in the minds of those early Christians, a semi-mythical city of unimaginable wealth and beauty, a city whose religion, in the minds of the early Christians, was nothing but materialistic idolatry. To them, Babylonian religion was filled with false gods and demons, its priests were black magicians.

John's vision talks of Babylon because the people of the early centuries of the Christian era felt they were living in a similar time, a time when the spirit had been prostituted to the flesh, a time when people turned away from God's call to salvation because they were too beguiled by the entice- ments of material beauty and wealth. A materialistic time par excellence! Much like our own time.

However, the new world to come is already implicit in that dour vision of what the world had been reduced to by its failure to honor the spirit. For if the present is Babylon— city of material wealth beyond compare—a new city is com- ing into existence, as much beyond Babylon as Babylon was beyond the small villages of mud-baked huts that preceded it. If the present is a Great Whore, an evil woman enticing man to the pleasures of the flesh at the expense of the spirit, the future must hold a new woman, who honors the spirit as well as the flesh. This will be a time when man's view of woman is fully differentiated, when the "other," represented to man by woman, has been fully explored and internalized.

Figure 20. In John's vision, fabled Babylon stands in contrast to the New Jerusalem to come, a contrast between superficial external riches and the eternal treasure within. ("Babylon Fallen," Gustave Doré, first published in *La Sainte Bible*, 1860.)

"Babylon the Great is fallen." "Alas, alas that great city." Yet the tears can soon turn into joy for, "the marriage of the Lamb is come, and his wife hath made herself ready." The new world is about to arise, when Christ—the god/human—will be fully joined with his bride—the feminine "other"—to form a new being for this new world. But first must come Armageddon.

CHAPTER 10

ARMAGEDDON AND THE MILLENNIUM

And he gathered them together into a place called in the Hebrew tongue Armageddon (16:16).

And I saw heaven opened, and behold a white horse; and he that sat upon him was called Faithful and True, and in righteousness he doth judge and make war. His eyes were as a flame of fire, and on his head were many crowns; and he had a name written, that no man knew, but he himself. . . . And out of his mouth goeth a sharp sword, that with it he should smite the nations: and he shall rule them with a rod of iron: and he treadeth the winepress of the fierceness and wrath of Almighty God. And he hath on his vesture and on his thigh a name written, KING OF KINGS, AND LORD OF LORDS (19:11–12, 15–16).

THE FINAL DAYS

The Christ who appears now is very different from the gentle, meek Christ of popular Christianity. This is a fierce Christ: "out of his mouth goeth a sharp sword, that with it should smite the nations, and he shall rule them with a rod of iron."

Earlier, we have seen how, with the creation of Adam, the struggle between spirit and body began. If it was a long, slow development from Adam to Christ, that is because it has taken mankind a very long time to evolve some way of resolving this strange amalgamation. The birth of Christ marked the first great milestone in this journey: the development of the full god/human. But it wasn't yet time for Christ to rule the world. Once he appeared, we could all change our view of ourselves and the universe. We could begin to slowly accept our divinity. However, this has been a very long development indeed. It took fourteen centuries from the time of Christ to the Renaissance before we realized that—as the only rational creature—we are the center of the universe, the measure of all about us. Can we even conceive of a Leonardo Da Vinci existing before the Renaissance?

By the 17th century, our vaunted intellect had stepped fully to center stage. Rene Descartes could proclaim: *cogito, ergo, sum* ("I think, therefore I am"), giving clear expression to the idea that the struggle between mind and body had already been won by the mind.

With the development of the scientific method in the 17th century, the way was prepared for the intellectual hubris that was the hallmark of the 19th century. Victorians saw themselves on the threshold of mastery over the universe. They felt that there were just a few remaining pieces of the puzzle to put into place, and then all would be understood, all the world under our dominion.

At the beginning of the 20th century, that view began to crumble. As just one example, consider physicist Werner Heisenberg's famous "uncertainty principle," one of the cornerstones of modern physics. Heisenberg theorized that we can know either the position or the momentum of an atomic particle, but not both. In order to find the particle's position, our observation changes the momentum; in order to discover the momentum, we change the particle's position. In other words, the observer cannot be separated from the observation, because the act of observation affects the experiment. This limitation is not a limitation of the equipment we use, but rather is built into the foundation of the universe.

In a logically ordered world, we could separate ourselves from the world and observe it. But we can't. In order to control the world, there has to be a world separate from us to be controlled. But there isn't. Heisenberg's world—our world—doesn't look much like that constructed world of science. In the world in which we all live, everything is interconnected, everything affects everything else. The world is a spider-web of immense complexity.

Heisenberg's "uncertainty principle" was one of the glimpses into the new world that awaits us that many could not accept. Much of this book has been an attempt to lead readers toward this new world. As I discussed in the opening pages of this book, those who can accept the truth of the new world—even if they don't fully understand it—need not fear.

However, at the time of Christ's ministry, it was still too early for Christ to be more than a symbol of what we could become, if we could accept the unity of all creation, a unity in which love formed the connections. But now, the time has come and a different Christ appears, a warrior Christ who must tear down the old to prepare the way for the new.

THE FATE OF THE "LUKE/WARM"

And I saw the beast, and the kings of the earth, and their armies, gathered together to make war against him that sat on the horse, and against his army. And the beast was taken, and with him the false prophet that wrought miracles before him, with which he deceived them that had received the mark of the beast, and them that worshiped his image. These both were cast alive into a lake of fire burning with brimstone. And the remnant were slain with the sword of him that sat upon

the horse, which sword proceeded out of his
mouth: and all the fowls were filled with their
flesh (19:19–21).

And I saw an angel come down from heaven,
having the key of the bottomless pit and a great
chain in his hand. And he laid hold on the
dragon, that old serpent, which is the Devil, and
Satan, and bound him a thousand years, And cast
him into the bottomless pit, and shut him up, and
set a seal upon him, that he should deceive the
nations no more, till the thousand years should be
fulfilled: and after that he must be loosed a little
season (20:1–3).

A great battle takes place with Christ and his forces arrayed
against the Dragon, the Beast, the False Prophet, and all
their worshippers. In other words, Christ battles against
those who still cling to the old, all who reduce the spirit to
the flesh, or degrade the flesh in the name of the spirit. This
is a battle which is really no battle at all, because the reactionary forces have long since lost. They have merely been
allowed their short period of rule. After the battle is over—
with Christ's forces, of course, triumphant—the Beast and
the False Prophet and those with the mark of the Beast are
"cast alive into a lake of fire burning with brimstone."

That still leaves Satan himself, and all those who were
not already dead as martyrs nor had been thrown into the
pit as worshippers of the Beast. In other words, those who
are like most of us: just ignoring the world around us, not
taking sides, not getting involved, just trying to take care of
our own needs. Readers may remember that near the beginning of the vision, when God gave his message to the seven
churches, the people most condemned were the Laodiceans.
Their crime was remaining lukewarm, avoiding the battle
between good and evil as if it did not concern them. Now
those lukewarm survivors are slain with the sword of him

that sat upon the horse [Christ, that is], which sword proceeded out of his mouth; and all the fowls were filled with
their flesh. Satan is bound and cast into the bottomless pit
to remain for a millennium.

These fowls had earlier been described as "fowls that
fly in the midst of heaven" (19:17). In other words, it is necessary for the body to die and be consumed by the spirit
before any further advance can be made. This is a theme that
has been echoed from the beginning of the Vision; e.g., the
Book of Life was only able to be opened by a "Lamb as it
had been slain" (5:6). Time after time in the Vision, mankind
is offered a chance to voluntarily die to its old definition.
Each time, some portion of mankind—the martyrs, the
"saved"—accept the message and are marked as God's faithful. Those who refuse to voluntarily die, die nevertheless,
slain each time by the impersonal forces under God's control—plagues, locusts, disease, fire, earthquakes, tornados.

OSIRIS, ISIS, SET AND HORUS

There is no way to avoid this death, the death that precedes
resurrection. In chapter 8, we discussed the Egyptian creation
myth of Ra and Isis. Bitten by the snake that Isis formed from
earth and Ra's spittle, Ra fell ill unto death. Only by giving
his "true name" to Isis could he be cured. But by doing so, he
was passing his power to Isis. This marked the passage from
a static world to an evolutionary world.

There's another Egyptian myth that speaks to us at this
point in the vision—the myth of Osiris, Isis, Set and Horus.
Osiris was husband and brother of Isis; i.e., those two functions of the Animus (i.e., the personified masculine characteristics within a woman) had not yet been differentiated.
This is the identical situation we discussed with the Anima
in the previous chapter.

Figure 21. The rule of Osiris and Isis marked our transition from bestiality to civilization; i.e., from an unconscious *participation mystique* with nature to the beginnings of ego consciousness. ("Osiris with his wife Isis and four children of Horus," reprinted from *The Gods of the Egyptians*.)

Osiris was identified by the other gods at birth as the "Universal Lord" who would rule wisely over the earth. According to Egyptian myth, before Osiris, people were savages who lived as animals among other animals. People were mere carnivores, hunting their daily food, which sometimes consisted of other people. Osiris in his mercy and wisdom brought culture to mankind. To the Egyptians, nearly everything identified with civilization was a gift from Osiris or his wife Isis.

Osiris began by eliminating cannibalism, thus separating mankind from their own bestiality. Wisely, he coupled that moral truth with the practical example of how they could have enough food for all by planting grain for food and grapes for wine. He taught people how to honor the gods who gave them this food from the earth with sacrifices, rituals and music. With an established agriculture, it was natural for people to settle by their fields, so he taught them how to live in cities. Having already taught religious laws and ritual so people could properly honor the gods, it was then natural to develop the social laws they needed to live in the close proximity of the cities.

In these endeavors he was assisted by his loving sister/wife Isis, who taught women how to grind the corn Osiris taught men to raise, how to spin flax and weave cloth. She even taught the men some of her great medical skills. Having established civilization in the heart of Egypt, Osiris proceeded to conquer the border territories. He did so, not with death and destruction, but with music and peace and harmony. Truly a great benefactor of mankind!

But all was not well in Egypt: his brother Set was jealous of Osiris, and Set was both violent and clever. Set ruled during Osiris' triumphant campaign and was wise enough not to attempt to change any of Osiris' policies. However, during this time Set considered how to overthrow Osiris. Following Osiris' triumphant return from his newly won territories, Set gave a great banquet. Osiris came, supposedly as the honored guest, not knowing that the other guests were all Set's henchmen.

At the banquet, a handsome, engraved chest was carried in and set before the admiring guests. Set announced that, as an entertainment, the chest would be given to whomever most closely fit inside. Osiris—being a good sport—lay down in the chest. Immediately, Set's henchmen nailed the chest closed, then threw it into the Nile River and watched it float away. The chest had become Osiris' coffin. Set was free to rule as he willed.

Isis mourned her husband deeply, then began searching for his coffin. After many travels, she found it and brought it back to Egypt, intending to use her great skills to bring Osiris back to life. Unfortunately, Set discovered what she had done and murdered Osiris a second time. This time, he cut the coffin into fourteen pieces, which he scattered over the face of the earth. But Isis still did not give up. She searched until she had found every piece of the coffin. She then reanimated her husband long enough for him to impregnate her. He then went peacefully to the Elysian Fields, where he reigned over the just dead.

The rest of the tale concerns the birth of Horus and his eventual war with Set. We will leave that part of the tale for the next chapter. It is enough for us now to deal with the clues which the myth can provide us at this key time in the vision. In the earlier story of Ra and Isis, it was clear that Ra had to yield his power if the world was ever to evolve and change from the static world of Ra's initial creation. But Osiris seems to present an almost idyllic picture of a god, whose every action benefits mankind. Thus the first message of the myth is that it is at the peak of development that the old has to die. This is exactly the message that most of us refuse to hear. After all, we insist, why should we change just when things are going well? When we refuse, the unconscious reacts in turn by making things progressively worse. But we still refuse: better the devil we know than the devil we don't.

Earlier in this chapter, we briefly traced a line of development from the Renaissance to the 20th century, a line of seeming progress. At the end of the 19th century, people felt much as mythological mankind must have felt in the Eden-like time when Osiris ruled. Similarly, it is just when we feel most convinced that we are on top of things, fully in charge of our lives, that we are likely to experience major changes.

The manner of Osiris' confinement and death is also particularly fitting (as his coffin was particularly fitting). Like the chest was for Osiris, our rigid self-definition is itself a coffin. In a time of major transition, we are carried along—without conscious knowledge or participation— toward our place of resurrection. If the change is great enough (like it was in the passage of eras from Osiris to Horus) the old has to be totally disassembled—broken down into its constituent parts—before it can be reassembled and reanimated. Similarly, we have seen in the 20th century how every major human institution has broken down: in science, art, religion, politics, you name it. Just like Osiris, we are bound within the coffin of our definition, a definition grown inadequate. In our individual experience, this corresponds to a disassociation of our normal personality. Our ego is a painfully won unity within, a unity among diversity, since in the unconscious many such personalities live. All the unacceptable, unexamined, undeveloped parts of our personality take personified form in the unconscious, held at bay by our egos' insistence on its primacy.

In normal times, we project those unconscious personalities out onto others who have some characteristics in common with our inner figures. We argue with them, relate to them, perhaps fall in love with them. As we get to know them better, we get to know those parts of our unconscious personality better, until finally we may incorporate those personality traits into our own identity. That's in normal time.

But when the change is more major, that method won't do. In such times, the ego isn't reacting to one new person-

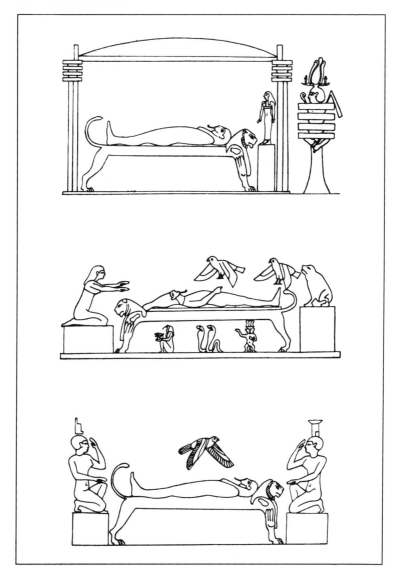

Figure 22. Just as unconsciousness has to yield to consciousness, so ego consciousness has to die in order for a still higher consciousness to develop. This latter transition is represented in Osiris's death and dismemberment by his brother Set. ("Funeral Bier of Osiris," reprinted from *The Gods of the Egyptians*.)

ality, it's reacting to a multitude of possible new personalities, a multitude with contradictory characteristics, no one of which is likely to be a solution to the conflict. At such a time, the ego must yield totally, without any knowledge of the eventual outcome. Within the unconscious, the conflict can then seek a new symbolic solution unencumbered by the arguments of the ego.

It is not a comfortable feeling to be split apart. All of us will do almost anything we can to avoid that dreaded situation. But it comes nevertheless. In the vision, Christ comes with a sword to cut us apart. Like Osiris's body—split into fourteen parts and scattered to the ends of the earth—those who still won't accept the new are cut apart and fed to the birds of the spirit.

In the vision, Satan is then imprisoned for a thousand years. Let's discuss this interim period—the Millennium— before we return in the next chapter to Osiris, Set, Isis, and Horus.

THE MILLENNIUM

This is one of the strangest parts of the Book of Revelation. Barely three paragraphs are spent on its description. It is a time when the martyrs, those who refused to honor the beast and suffered thereby, are resurrected and live in honor with Christ for a thousand years.

> Blessed and holy is he that hath part in the first resurrection: on such the second death hath no power, but they shall be priests of God and of Christ, and shall reign with him a thousand years (20:6).

It is common these days for people to describe themselves as "born-again" Christians. All spiritual traditions know that one must die to one's old life, suffer, then be reborn. In large part, Jungian psychology is an attempt to describe how to go through that necessary transformation. In many ways, the whole Book of Revelation is an attempt to capture some picture of what that death and rebirth will be like. The Tibetan Book of the Dead, the Egyptian Book of the Dead, the Hopi prophesies, on and on throughout the ages, wise men have tried to capture this passage for us. The Bible is trying to tell us that those who are willing to struggle in their own lives to find some individual answer to this great passage into a new stage of consciousness—those who voluntarily submit to death and transformation—need not fear the general shift of consciousness. They will be the "priests of God and Christ" who will lead others to an understanding of the new world that awaits us all.

At the end of the Millennium, Satan is released and once more roams the world, creating death and destruction, luring the world to a sense of false pride and security in his old ways. But if all have already been killed and eaten by the heavenly birds, who is left?

In order to answer that, we have to look again at those who "were slain with the sword . . . which sword proceeded out of his [i.e., Christ's] mouth." That is a very strange image which I didn't address directly except to contrast a fierce Christ with a meek Christ. Christ is given a very specific title for this battle: "his name is called The Word of God." So not only is this a Christ for the end of the era of the god/human—a Christ ready now to do battle—but this is Christ as representative of the Word of God (as in "the Word was made flesh and dwelt amongst us"). A very special view of Christ, indeed.

We have already seen the importance of the word many times before in this book. In the Egyptian creation myth, the light of Ra's eyes created the world around him, and the light and the word were one and the same. When Ra told Isis his secret name, he gave up all his power. In the biblical creation myth, after God created Adam, Adam's power came from the word, for it was Adam who named the beasts of the field.

Mankind's attempt to consciously understand the divinity discovered within led to an overestimation of logic and intellect. In our understandable confusion, we reduced the Spirit to intellect, the Word to mere words. But eventually words had to come to an end; words themselves had to lead us to a point beyond logical definition. We have seen that that time came at the beginning of the 20th century. Since then, we have struggled to rid ourselves of this new knowledge, but in the words God addressed to the people of the city of Philadelphia early in the Book of Revelation: "I have set before thee an open door, and no man can shut it."

Christ as the Word of God had to appear and destroy all the false words of Satan and the Anti-Christ and his False Prophet. He did so in the great battle that left Satan in the pit, waiting out the Millennium. But God is not only Logos, not just the Word; that is only one aspect of God: the masculine aspect. And that masculine time is ending. It is time for the Marriage of the Lamb with his new Bride, a joining of masculine and feminine into one being.

So, in answer to my question of who is left if all have already been killed and eaten by the birds of Heaven, just imagine that once again the Book of Revelation will show us the same battle in a different way, in order to teach us a different lesson. One lesson was to stress the triumph of Logos over mere logic, the victory of the Word over mere words. Now we must learn of a different victory—the final victory.

CHAPTER 11

THE NATURE OF EVIL

And when the thousand years are expired, Satan shall be loosed out of his prison; And shall go out to deceive the nations which are in the four quarters of the earth, Gog and Magog, to gather them together to battle: the number of whom is as the sand of the sea.

And they went up on the breadth of the earth, and compassed the camp of the saints about, and the beloved city: and fire came down from God out of heaven, and devoured them.

And the devil that deceived them was cast into the lake of fire and brimstone, where the beast and the false prophet are, and shall be tormented day and night for ever and ever (20:7–10).

A MANDALA OF GOOD AND EVIL

To many people, this passage appears to describe the destruction of the world by a nuclear war between two great superpowers like the United States and the Soviet Union. But my interest here is less in the possibility that this great vision from the unconscious might actually take such an outer form, than in what it conveys of the inner state of the world. In this image of battle, we have a profound symmetry: four quarters, two opposing armies, "compassed"

Figure 23. When ego consciousness becomes fragmented, a new wholeness forms around the Self. In a wide variety of cultures, this inner
wholeness is represented by symmetric pictures called mandalas. This
mandala was painted by C. G. Jung. Reprinted from *Jung in Bild and
Wort*. (Solothur, Switzerland, Walter Verlag, 1977; published in the USA
by Princeton University Press as *Jung in Word and Image*). Copyright ©
The Estate of C. G. Jung. Used by kind permission.

about the saints. Carl Jung was interested in these symmetric creations of the spirit, called "mandalas." We have already encountered many in the vision, though I haven't previously identified them as mandalas. Now it's time.

I've talked about the Self from many aspects already. Now we need to see the Self as the ultimate centering pattern in nature, the ultimate balance. Our era is a failure in many ways, but above all it lacks balance. (As we discussed in Chapter 1, the Hopis have a phrase for our modern world: *Koyaanisqatsi*, Hopi for "world out of balance"). We are continually thrown from one extreme to another, from doom-filled depression to wild elation. One moment the world is coming to an end because we have greedily consumed all of our natural resources, the next moment we blithely talk of atomic fusion supplying endless power. Even the idea of balance and stability seems like a dream from the past; the world we know is a world in perpetual motion.

But all of us have felt a place deep inside us, where all those opposites cancel out, and peace is found (in the words of 20th century poet and philosopher George Santayana: "Heaven is to be at peace with things"). All of us have experienced moments of transcendence in our lives, moments when there was no opposition, no strife. The deepest teachings of all spiritual traditions are attempts to find that place inside ourselves, to help us become aware that it exists, so that we may live our lives from that holy center.

Jung found that people of widely varied cultures have spontaneously attempted to capture their deepest spiritual feelings in visual symmetric patterns—mandalas. He found mandalas appeared in the dreams of his patients at times when they were desperately attempting to find a new center, a new balance. In that light, consider what it means when John's vision presents us with a mandala formed by the forces of evil on the outside and the saints and their "beloved city" in the center.

The saints and the "beloved city" form a core of Goodness, a center for the new life to come. These saints are the martyrs who willingly died for Christ, who gave up their personal lives as individuals to serve the new vision. The vision has already said that they will have nothing to fear. Now the reactionary forces of the world form an evil mandala, threatening to engulf the last vestige of the Good. At that point "fire came down from God out of heaven, and devoured them."

Evil has to reach a peak; it has to reveal itself as a thing in itself. In the vision, Gog is pitted against Magog: evil against evil. Evil comes from all four quarters of the earth, it encircles the Good. This is very different from the easier portrait of evil as the absence of good that most of us have been taught in our secular age. But the vision shows us that there is a point beyond which the evil cannot go, a center that transcends earthly good and evil. The saints in the middle are not merely good: they are Good (in the sense that they have died and transcended all such opposites).

THE NATURE OF EVIL

No single event in modern history has better exemplified evil than the Holocaust. Perhaps no one has recorded their personal response to the Holocaust more movingly than the late Primo Levi. Levi recently committed suicide by throwing himself down the stairs of the apartment building in which he lived. In recent years, his sadness had grown over the revisionist histories that tried to define the Holocaust away: the Holocaust that Levi had lived through as a concentration camp prisoner, and recorded in his books.

His death produced an astonishing outpouring of emotion throughout the world. In a wide variety of magazines, writers asked whether his suicide negated the affirmation of his work, an affirmation that gave so many comfort during difficult times? They struggled with the question of why Levi could survive the concentration camps and write with joy and deep understanding of his experience, yet not be able to survive in our own (admittedly troubled) times. Can the world now be even worse for a person of sensitivity like Levi than it was in Hitler's concentration camps? These are not easy questions.

Levi was both a writer of world class and a chemist. In the *Periodic Table*, he brought both together in the service of his wartime memories of his native Italy and later in Auschwitz. In 1869, Russian chemist Dmitri Mendeleey discovered how to arrange the chemical elements in a table which brought order to the seeming chaos of the elements. In effect, he was able to intuit the inner structure of the atom three decades before it was to be revealed by physics. Levi carefully selected twenty-one chemical elements and told a story, usually autobiographical and drawn from his wartime experiences, about each element. He attempted, like Mendeleey, to discover the underlying order hidden in chaos, as if that knowledge could transmute horror into understanding. And somehow, in Levi's hands, it does! Here is Primo Levi on his efforts to learn how to steal in order to survive in Auschwitz:

> If you do not begin as a child, learning to steal is not easy; it had taken me several months before I could repress the moral commandments and acquire the necessary techniques, and at a certain point I realized (with a flash of laughter and a pinch of satisfied ambition) that I was reliving— me, a respectable little university graduate—the involution-evolution of a famous respectable dog, a Victorian, Darwinian dog who is deported and becomes a thief in order to live in his Klondike Lager—the great Buck of *The Call of the Wild*. I stole like him and like the fox's: at every favorable opportunity but with sly cunning and without exposing myself. I STOLE EVERYTHING

EXCEPT THE BREAD OF MY COMPANIONS
[author's emphasis].[1]

How can Levi's later suicide in any way deny that triumph of the human spirit? Life is long and all of us tire. But here he recorded something very valuable for all of us: evil at its peak can lead to new vitality and strength if we can only find a center within, a place of wholeness. In Levi's case, it taught him to steal like a wild animal. In another case, it might teach a wild animal how to adapt to civilization. The outer manifestation is unimportant, but once awakened, that center always brings strength and joy in adversity.

THE FINAL JUDGMENT AND HORUS AND SET

> And I saw the dead, small and great, stand before God; and the books were opened: and another book was opened, which is the book of life: and the dead were judged out of those things which were written in the books, according to their works. . . . And whosoever was not found written in the book of life was cast into the lake of fire (20:12, 15).

Finally we have arrived at Judgment Day. All who have ever died are resurrected and called before the throne for judgment. The Book of Life is opened, wherein the lives of all are recorded. Each is judged and "whosoever was not written in the book of life was cast into the lake of fire." This is the same book that we learned early in the vision could only be opened by a "Lamb as it had been slain." Now all are dead and all will be judged.

---

[1] Primo Levi, *The Periodic Table* (New York: Schoken Books, 1984), p. 140.

It is appropriate at this time to return to the story of Osiris, Isis, Set, and Horus, which will itself end in a trial and a final judgment. Isis had reanimated Osiris in order to have him impregnate her, before he retired to the Elysian Fields. Isis gave birth to Horus, then used her magical powers to protect him from Set until he could grow to manhood and avenge his father's murder. Osiris returned from the dead periodically to watch over his son and teach him the skills of battle he would later need to compete successfully with Set. When Horus had grown to manhood, he warred against Set. Their war was fought so bitterly that finally the other gods called a council to rule for once and for all over their dispute.

At the trial, Set tried all of his cunning, arguing that Horus could not be the true heir of Osiris since Osiris was already dead before Horus was conceived. This was rather like a murderer who killed a father then argued that the orphaned son was really a bastard since he knew that the father wasn't there to defend his son's paternity. However, Osiris was a god, not a human. He appeared in his reconstituted form before the gods, and authenticated his son's lineage. The gods then accepted Horus as the rightful heir of Osiris and condemned Set for his multiple crimes. Horus became the god/king of Egypt who embodied himself in the succession of Pharaohs. [Note: The reader should be aware that there are many different versions of the story of Osiris, Isis, Horus, and Set, just as there are many versions of every myth and fairy tale.]

As in the first part of the myth, which we discussed in the previous chapter, this second part gives us some clues into the nature of the mighty transition we are encountering in the vision. Osiris was just and good, yet he had to die and yield to his evil brother Set. Thus it is just when some fine development has reached its peak that it has to yield. And it has to yield to the opposite, a force which is initially seen as evil.

When Osiris was reassembled and reanimated, he didn't then continue his just reign. Instead he retired to the Elysian fields where he could reign over the dead. His reanimation

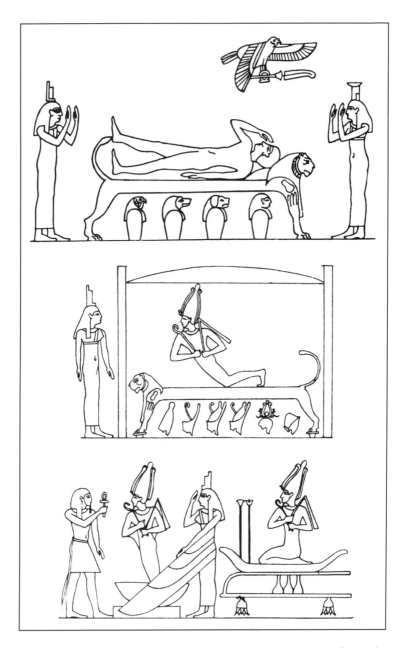

Figure 24. After Osiris was split into pieces and scattered over the earth, Isis found all the pieces and reanimated Osiris, so that he could impregnate her with the new life which would be born as Horus. ("The Resurrection of Osiris," reprinted from *The Gods of the Egyptians*.)

was only to impregnate Isis with his eventual successor—Horus. In other words, the new life is not merely a different presentation of the old, it is truly new: Horus is a different being than Osiris. When a caterpillar dies and forms a cocoon about itself, its entire body structure is broken down into its constituent molecules. There is no caterpillar at that point, it exists only as a solution—and a plan contained somehow within the solution! The plan reforms the molecules into a butterfly.

Yet, paradoxically enough, the plan for the butterfly has to already be contained in the caterpillar or there would be no butterfly. Child psychologist Jean Piaget carefully demonstrated that infants are not the blank slates "on which experience will write its tale" that behaviorists would have them be. Piaget showed how infants contain an enormous amount of cognitive skills, that are activated at appropriate times in their development.

One famous example is the cognitive concept that quantity is independent of the shape and size of the container. Before children reach the age when that concept can be understood, if you present them with milk in a short, squatty container, then pour it into a tall, narrow container, they will insist there is now more milk. Poured back into the shorter container, they'll say there is less milk. They simply can not yet understand that the amount of milk doesn't vary. When they reach the right age, they do understand—it's no longer a puzzle to them.

THE LIMITS OF LOGIC

When Set pleaded his case before the other gods, he used all his wiles, arguing that Horus could not be the son of Osiris, since Osiris was dead before Horus was conceived. Logically, this seems an unanswerable argument. However, when Osiris actually appeared and recognized Horus as his

Figure 25. In many ways, Horus is a prefiguration of Christ. He represents the next stage after ego consciousness. ("Horus, the son of Isis and Osiris," reprinted from *The Gods of the Egyptians*.)

son before the gods, Set's argument was revealed to be base-less. So it is when words and logic finally have to confront reality. Words and logic can lead us to strange conclusions, conclusions that have little or nothing to do with reality.

As we have already seen, it is the isolation of thinking from feeling, the masculine from the feminine, Logos from Eros that lies at the root of the problems of our day. Logic in itself is insufficient to deal with bigger issues. Logic is insufficient to use in reaching a "final judgment" on reality. If the reader will forgive me, I would like to take another detour to demonstrate this, a detour through the history of mathematics.

> There is something peculiar, one might even say mysterious, about numbers. . . . If . . . a group of objects is deprived of every single one of its properties or characteristics, there still remains, at the end, its number, which seems to indicate that number is something irreducible. . . . [something which] helps more than anything else to bring order into the chaos of appearances. . . . It may well be the most primitive element of order in the human mind. . . . we [can] define number psychologically as an archetype of order which has become conscious.[2]

Few people are forced to confront such epistemological questions in the course of their lives: life is concrete, not abstract. But mathematicians live in an abstract world which is to them fully as real as the physical world. Mathematical problems don't often lend themselves to concrete description or resolution. While mathematicians are as

---

[2] C. G. Jung: *The Collected Works of C. G. Jung,* trans. R. F. C. Hull, Bollingen Series XX. Vol. 8: *The Structure and Dynamics of the Psyche* (Princeton, NJ: Princeton University Press, 1960, 1969), ¶ 870.

Figure 26. At some point, in order to gain proper perspective, it becomes necessary to view our human nature from an objective, abstract place. Jung felt that number was the primary archetype of order, from which all other archetypes evolved. (From *Perspective*, Jan Vredeman de Vrias. New York: Dover, 1968.)

"worldly" as anyone else, their "worlds" are abstract creations (or are they discoveries?) such as algebra, calculus, topology, or number theory. Mathematicians understand the nature and laws of their mathematical worlds as thoroughly as a geologist understands the world of rock formations, a botanist the world of plants. However, in contrast to the physically observable worlds of geologists and botanists, mathematical worlds seemingly exist only as a shared agreement among mathematicians as to what constitutes those worlds.

> Now if we conceive numbers as having been discovered, and not merely invented as an instrument for counting, then on account of their mythological nature they belong to the realm of "godlike" human and animal figures and are just as archetypal as they. Unlike these, however, they are "real" in the sense that they are encountered in the realm of experience as quantities and thus form the bridge between the tangible, physical world and the imaginary. Though the latter is unreal, it is "real" in so far as it works; i.e., has an effect on us.[3]

Twentieth-century mathematician Kurt Gödel came to the same belief as Jung: the belief that number was the primary archetype which underlay reality. Gödel stood at the end of a long line of development of mathematical thought, which led to increasing rigor and abstraction. This line of thought received its first clear articulation twenty-three hundred years ago when a Greek mathematician named Euclid collected and systematized the complete body of geometric knowledge into a single work, later termed *Euclid's Elements* or *The Elements of Euclidian Geometry*.

---

[3] C. G. Jung: *The Collected Works of C. G. Jung*, trans. R. F. C. Hull, Bollingen Series XX. Vol. 10: *Civilization in Transition* (Princeton, NJ: Princeton University Press, 1964, 1970), ¶ 776.

Euclid's Elements became one of the most famous and significant books ever written. It consisted of a small number of definitions (such as "point," "line," "perpendicular," etc.) and ten axioms (i.e., self-evident truths). From the definitions and axioms, Euclid derived all of geometry. This method of developing a full body of mathematical knowledge from a small number of definitions and axioms later came to be called the "axiomatic method." Geometry provided a systematic method of solving problems that were more complex than could be solved by simple direct measurement in the physical world. An abstract system of thought could thus reveal hidden knowledge about the physical world. Why should this be possible? Jung says that it occurs because:

> . . . [Numbers] do not only count and measure, and are not merely quantitative; they also make qualitative statements and are therefore a mysterious something midway between myth and reality, partly discovered and partly invented. Equations, for instance, that were invented as pure mathematical formulae have subsequently proved to be formulations of the quantitative behavior of physical things.[4]

The next great step in mathematical rigor came almost two thousand years later, when 17th-century mathematician and philosopher Rene Descartes discovered analytic geometry. Analytic geometry translated points on a plane into coordinates: two numbers indicating the horizontal and vertical distance a point lay from a fixed origin. With points translated into numbers, lines, and curves could then be described using algebraic formulas. With this increasing degree of abstraction, algebraic mathematical techniques could be used to more simply attack problems which were

---

[4] Carl Jung, *The Collected Works*, Vol. 10, ¶ 777.

overly complex or even irresolvable within geometry. Still a further step toward power through abstraction.

Less than fifty years after Descartes' invention of analytic geometry, Isaac Newton and Baron Gottfried Wilhelm von Leibnitz independently developed "calculus." Calculus gave mathematicians the ability to measure the previous immeasurable: irregular shapes, volumes, surfaces, etc., and perhaps even more importantly: movement across time. Geometry "abstracted" the elemental symbols of physical reality: points, lines, curves, etc. Geometricians then could manipulate the symbols and later translate them back into physical reality. With analytic geometry, the points and lines of geometry were further abstracted into numbers and formulas. Being still more abstract than the geometric elements, they were still more easily manipulated. Calculus brought time and irregularity within the abstract mathematical model.

Spurred on by the power of abstraction, in the late 19th century, mathematicians attempted to turn mathematics into a totally formal system which concerned itself with the meaningless manipulation of contentless signs. They had forgotten that their mathematical symbols were not empty signs; rather they were either abstractions from reality or (as is part of our thesis in this chapter) they were preexistent and essentially indefinable forms. Consider what actually happened when mathematicians abstracted symbols like "points" and "lines" from reality. Since reality is continuous, any such abstraction "stuffs" more of reality into the symbol than can ever be readily understood. A symbol, when amplified back into all the things it supposedly stands for, is always endless. The first mathematicians who looked at physical reality and saw points and lines were actually making a great mental leap: discovering symbols where previously we had only seen nature.

But mathematicians aren't philosophers. Their goal was to formalize the axiomatic method by removing any relationship between the physical world and their abstract definitions and axioms, then to extend this method to all of mathematics. However, as they took on this mighty task, they came to realize that even mathematics' most elementary field—arithmetic—stood on very shaky logical ground. Unless they could prove that arithmetic was both "complete" and "consistent," what had they really accomplished by their formalization? By "complete," they meant that any true arithmetic statement could be derived from the definitions and axioms of arithmetic. By "consistent," mathematicians meant that it was not possible to derive both a true statement and its opposite from the same definitions and axioms.

As incredible as it might sound, in 1931 Kurt Gödel proved that their task was impossible. He demonstrated that any mathematical system at least as "rich" as arithmetic, was either incomplete or inconsistent. Initially Gödel's proof was viewed by many mathematicians as a disaster for mathematics: Gödel had destroyed the possibility of ever developing a fully complete and consistent body of logical thought (for Gödel's argument was in no way limited to mathematics per se). Today many mathematicians and logicians would insist that his results, while true, were anomalous: logical systems are complete and consistent except for a few meaningless paradoxical statements such as the one Gödel used to demonstrate his conclusion.

In contrast to this reductionist view, I would like to argue that Gödel did not reduce the world with his proof, he vastly extended it. He proved that the world is infinitely richer (literally *infinitely* richer) than any logical system. Systems of thought (such as mathematics, physics, biology, etc.), which the proponents of formalism had tried to present as merely tautological developments of a finite set of definitions and axioms, are instead revealed to be infinitely extendable amplifications of symbols. Mathematics (and, by extension, science, art, life itself) is not concerned with the meaningless manipulation of empty signs. Rather it concerns the mysterious properties inherent in unknowable symbols. Every number, every word, every concept, every image is symbolic—and therefore capable of being end-lessly amplified. Because of this, mathematics, as our most abstract discovery, is capable of being amplified to discuss nearly anything else we care to discuss.

I hope readers will excuse such a long trip through the history of mathematics, but it is directly applicable to our situation. Logic in itself is insufficient to deal with the greater issues. Judgment requires feeling as well as logic. As in so many other areas, Jung took a lead in this recognition as well. He recognized "feeling" as a function of the mind, independent of "thinking." Thinking defines something, tells us "what it is," while feeling evaluates something, tells us "what it's worth." It's feeling, not thinking, which lets us conclude that something is good or bad, right or wrong. That's why the gods decide against Set. He uses logical arguments to try and prove that Horus could not possibly be Osiris' son. Yet Osiris delivers an emotional defense of his son's parentage and the gods believe him, not Set. Judg-ment comes from feeling, not thinking.

The Final Judgment is a "feeling" evaluation, not a "thinking" evaluation. It isn't concerned with logical loop-holes, with elaborate definition, it's concerned with feelings because only feelings are complex enough to deal with the bigger issues of life. Gödel and Jung believed that num-bers—the seeming apotheosis of logic—were the primary archetype of the universe. Yet, as Gödel demonstrated, numbers are not the product of logic, but of feeling and intuition.

It is not that feeling is inherently superior to thinking, nor that intuitive knowledge is superior to detailed sensory knowledge. Rather balance is needed, and balance is found in the recognition of human limitation. While Adam was made in God's image, he was also one with the animals. While Christ was God, he was also human. It is in accepting our humanity, with its concomitant need to struggle between our poles, that we can find a way to a higher place

𝕿𝖍𝖊 𝖂𝖔𝖓𝖉𝖊𝖗𝖘 𝖔𝖋 𝖙𝖍𝖊 𝕴𝖓𝖛𝖎𝖘𝖎𝖇𝖑𝖊 𝖂𝖔𝖗𝖑𝖉.

OBSERVATIONS

As well *Historical* as *Theological*, upon the NATURE, the NUMBER, and the OPERATIONS of the

DEVILS.

Accompany'd with,

I. Some Accounts of the Grievous Molestations, by DÆ-MONS and WITCHCRAFTS, which have lately annoy'd the Countrey; and the Trials of some eminent *Malefactors* Executed upon occasion thereof: with several Remarkable *Curiosities* therein occurring.

II. Some Counsils, Directing a due Improvement of the terrible things, lately done, by the Unusual & Amazing Range of EVIL SPIRITS, in Our Neighbourhood: & the methods to prevent the *Wrongs* which those *Evil Angels* may intend against all sorts of people among us, especially in Accusations of the Innocent.

III. Some Conjectures upon the great EVENTS, likely to befall, the WORLD in General, and NEW EN-GLAND in Particular; as also upon the Advances of the TIME, when we shall see BETTER DAYES.

IV. A short Narrative of a late Outrage committed by a knot of WITCHES in *Swedeland*, very much Resembling, and so far Explaining, *That* under which our parts of *America* have laboured!

V. THE DEVIL DISCOVERED: In a Brief Discourse upon those TEMPTATIONS, which are the more Ordinary *Devices* of the Wicked One.

By 𝕮𝖔𝖙𝖙𝖔𝖓 𝕸𝖆𝖙𝖍𝖊𝖗.

Boston Printed by *Benj. Harris* for *Sam. Phillips.* 1693.

Figure 27. In every age, the evil we are unwilling to confront within, is expressed without in awful atrocities. (Title page from one of Cotton Mather's witch-hunt pamphlets, Boston 1693.)

which is not at the expense of part of our soul. Progress at the expense of losing part of our essential being is not progress at all. The experience of the Nazis, with their grand ideals, should certainly have taught us that.

SURVIVING EVIL

Earlier in this chapter, I described how, in *The Periodic Table*, Primo Levi demonstrated that the periodic table of chemical elements was alive and vital, constructed from human dreams and human failings. In contrast, the Nazis and Fascists thought themselves paradigms of order and logic. Mussolini is still praised by closet fascists for "making the trains run on time." Hitler's Gestapo prided themselves on their discipline and order. Only a mania for order and structure could have created a system of death which operated so efficiently and so impersonally. Hannah Arendt taught us the "banality" of the Nazis. That banality was the result of allowing themselves to be cut off from the profound depths of human emotion. The executioners could blithely gas people during the day and go home at night to their family and children.

There is an economy to the psyche. Whatever is lacking in consciousness is compensated for in the unconscious. When the Nazis consciously praised purity and light, then primitive feelings of impurity and darkness arose in the unconscious in compensation. They couldn't have their master race without a compensatory hatred of anyone who didn't fit into that pattern: Jews, Poles, Gypsies, etc. Too much light brings forth the darkness. We are humans, with human limitations, not supermen or superwomen.

Levi was always haunted by the fact that those who, like himself, survived the Holocaust, might have been the worst of those there. They scratched and clawed and found any way possible to survive, except for condemning their fellow beings (remember Levi's own description: "I stole everything except the bread from my companions"). Levi was wrong in accusing himself. They weren't collaborating in the evil of their captors. They were human! Like humans, they fought with every resource available to them, little as it was. Their captors were no longer human, they had been reduced to robots.

We Americans would love to believe that life is simpler than Levi and his companions found it to be. We believe in a Wild West code where the Good Guys and the Bad Guys have a showdown and the good guys win. If evil was that weak, there would be no need for an Armageddon, for a final judgment. Sometimes it is enough merely to survive evil, to separate oneself from evil.

CHAPTER 12

THE NEW JERUSALEM

And I saw a new heaven and a new earth: for the first heaven and the first earth were passed away; and there was no more sea. And I John saw the holy city, new Jerusalem, coming down from God out of heaven, prepared as a bride adorned for her husband (21:1–2).

Ours is a brand new world of all allatonceness. "Time" has ceased, "space" has vanished. We now live in a global village . . . a simultaneous happening. We are back in acoustic space. We have begun again to structure the primordial feeling, the tribal feelings from which a few centuries of literary divorced us.[1]

A NEW UNITY

Finally, we arrive at the end of all strife and the descent from heaven to earth of the New Jerusalem. We have taken a long twisting path through the Book of Revelation to arrive here, but there is still much to learn in the description of the holy city. John says that "I saw a new heaven and a new earth, for the first heaven and the first earth were passed away, and there was no more sea." Heaven lies

---

[1] Marshall McLuhan and Quentin Fiore, *The Medium Is the Massage* (New York: Bantam, 1967), p. 63.

Figure 28. With the appearance of the New Jerusalem, the old distinctions between material and spiritual, within and without, disappear. ("The New Jerusalem," Gustave Doré, first published in *La Sainte Bible*, 1860.)

above—the world of the spirit. Earth below, the world of the body. The sea connects the two.

The sea is the "mother of life," where all life started, where the distinctions between plant and animal are less clearcut than we find them on land. The sea is deep and dark, and there the first organic molecules formed, there the first simple proteins, nucleonic acids, DNA itself came into being. Beyond that material sea that holds so many mysteries yet, is a deeper spiritual sea: the unconscious. The unconscious—an even greater mystery—gave birth to all the archetypes we experience in dreams and visions (and in our everyday lives), whether we recognize them or not.

There is a mighty teaching here of the new world of consciousness that awaits us. In that world, there is no need for an unconscious ("there was no more sea") that is neither spirit nor matter. There is only a new spirit and a new matter. What would that mean? After all, the unconscious forms the connection between spirit and matter. This could only be because spirit and matter would now be seen as already—inherently—one. We will have to reserve until later in this chapter an understanding of how that can be.

> John saw the holy city, new Jerusalem, coming down from God out of heaven, prepared as a bride adorned for her husband (21:2).

This is no longer the seemingly endless stage of the development of the god/human; that task has been completed. Now there is to be a mating of opposites, a merging of masculine and feminine, spirit and body, mind and matter into a single entity. That much we have expected from much which we have already discussed in this book.

> And I heard a great voice out of heaven saying, Behold, the tabernacle of God is with men, and he will dwell with them, and they shall be his peo-

ple, and God himself shall be with them, and be their God (21:3).

Here we have an even stronger statement that the days of opposition are over. God himself will no longer be separate from mankind, because mankind resolved the god / human problem that has bedeviled him since mankind came into existence as a conscious entity. Then the New Jerusalem herself descends from heaven to earth.

A GREAT CRYSTALLINE STRUCTURE

. . . her light was like unto a stone most precious,
even like a jasper stone, clear as crystal (21:11).

The New Jerusalem is being compared to a crystal. You may recall that in chapter 5, we mentioned that "Jung was fond of making an analogy between the formation of symbols in the unconscious and the formation of crystals in a saturated solution." Consider the nature of a crystal. A crystal is a pattern that repeats itself endlessly. No matter where you look in a crystal, you find the same atoms in the same physical arrangement. What is even more magical is that the crystalline pattern that grows so readily is already contained in the combinations of atoms themselves. Put the right atoms together and, because they are limited in their possibilities of combination by their internal structure, they will form a crystal.

Think about that: no one atom contains the plan for a crystal, but all in combination do. That's the way Jung saw the manifestation of archetypes in outer reality: as patterns waiting to take form when the right elements came together. Konrad Lorenz' baby goose couldn't have known what a mother goose should look like; certainly Lorenz didn't look like a goose. The Mother archetype contained within the baby goose was an empty pattern waiting to take form.

It's helpful to think of archetypes as having two forms of manifestation: as symbols they take concrete visual form in dreams, myths, art, etc. As instincts, they take concrete form in outer behaviors. Archetypes are a new concept for most of us, instincts an old discarded concept. Instincts are not very popular today, with our overemphasis on behavioral answers for everything. Gregory Bateson wittily described "instinct" as "our name for anything which we know absolutely nothing about." If we think about instinct at all, we never really bother to consider what a mystery an instinct really is.

Consider research on identical twins, separated at an early age. When such twins are reunited as adults, the most astonishing similarities are found. For example, the Lewis brothers were identical twins. Separated as babies, when they met again as adults, they found their likes and dislikes, and even the actual events of their lives in amazing concordance. Let me mention only one small item here: as children, both had a dog as a pet, and both named it Toy! Now where could there be an "instinct" that would determine that when a little boy gets old enough to have a pet dog, he will name it "Toy"?[2]

Terry Conolly and Margaret Richardson were also separated as infants. In 1960, neither of them even knew that she had a twin sister, yet both married on exactly the same day in 1960, within an hour of each other. What sort of creatures are we humans if we are born into the world already containing a code that either knows the moment in our lives when we will marry, or (more likely) triggers us to marry at just that time?

We always have the illusion of seeing the old environment when we really see the new. The cliche is that which is pervasive, accepted totally

---

[2] Examples are from Peter Watson's *Twins: An Uncanny Relationship* (New York: Viking, 1982).

in the present environment. Archetype is the preceding environment. The new environment is constantly pushing the old into archetypal form.[3]

To the same extent that a human is more complex than a rock, archetypes are more complex than crystals. New Jerusalem is pictured as an enormous crystalline structure, "a jasper, clear as a crystal." That's the world that awaits us, an incredibly complex archetypal pattern, like a crystal infinitely replicatible, yet like our lives, infinitely varied.

THE NUMBER TWELVE

And had a wall great and high, and had twelve gates, and at the gates twelve angels, and names written thereon, which are the names of the twelve tribes of the children of Israel: On the east three gates; on the north three gates; on the south three gates; and on the west three gates. And the wall of the city had twelve foundations, and in them the names of the twelve apostles of the Lamb.

And he that talked with me had a golden reed to measure the city, and the gates thereof, and the wall thereof. And the city lieth foursquare, and the length is as large as the breadth: and he measured the city with the reed, twelve thousand furlongs. The length and the breadth and the height of it are equal. And he measured the wall thereof, an hundred and forty and four cubits, according to the measure of a man, that is, of the angel (21:12–17).

---

[3] Marshall McLuhan quoted from an article in *Life Magazine*, February 28, 1986, cited in *"The Perfect Pitch"* (newsletter), July 22, 1985.

I've talked a great deal about the significance of numbers already, about sevens and twos and fours. This new world is built around twelves, with twelve gates and twelves angels protecting the gates, and the names of the twelve tribes of Israel. A city with twelve foundations, a city twelve furlongs long and wide and high: a city made up of the concept "twelve"!

There are twelve signs of the zodiac, representing twelve different varieties of human personality. There are twelve major gods in each of the Greek, Roman, and Norse traditions. There are usually twelve major events in a hero's life; e.g., twelve episodes in Moses' life, twelve adventures of Ulysses, twelve labors of Hercules, twelve stations in Christ's Passion.

Twelve is the most divisible number: it can be split into halves, thirds, fourths, or sixths. Because of this divisibility, many mathematicians throughout the ages have proposed that a new numeric system should be developed, in which twelve is the base, not ten.

The New Jerusalem reflects that divisibility, having four sides, each with three gates, to make twelves gates in all. As a combination of three and four, it appears to be both static (i.e., four as a symbol of wholeness) and moving (i.e., three as a symbol of motion and change). For the latter, picture a wheel with three legs equally spaced around it (a common medieval picture). Such a wheel seems inherently designed to roll onto one leg, then another and another. On the other hand, four seems solid and stable—like a square, equally stable on any of its four sides, with no tendency to shift. Thus the city is inherently stable, since it's built with four sides, yet capable of movement and change, since there are three ways in and out of each side.

Jung expressed the whole problem of our age as the conflict between three and four. Our religion is based on the trinity of Father, Son and Holy Ghost. Such a formulation lacks the fourth necessary for stability. Jung saw the fourth developing out of the feminine, as we have already examined at some length. If our time is a passage from a time of three to a time of four, then twelve perfectly expresses a harmony between the two.

John's vision is stretching the limits of the collective symbols available at that point in history in order to try and express the strange qualities of the new world to come. He has already said there will be heaven and earth, but no land. The city itself is an enormous crystal, like a crystal always the same, yet capable of growth. The city is built on twelves, not tens to reflect its unusual combination of inherent stability yet its possibility for growth.

Nearly two millennia have passed since John's vision. Archetypes have slowly evolved in the unconscious. New symbols are starting to emerge to reflect the archetypal change in the universe. Let's now turn to one such symbol: the holographic universe, which neurophysiologist Karl Pribram and physicist David Boehm have theorized is the world in which we all live.

KARL PRIBRAM'S HOLOGRAPHIC WORLD

Karl Pribram is one of the most highly regarded neurophysiologists in the world, perhaps the single most highly regarded. He began his work as a neurosurgeon in the 1940's under Karl Lashley: the most eminent neurophysiologist of his era. Lashley was searching—unsuccessfully—for "engrams" (i.e. the localized sites of specific memories in the brains). Famed biologist Rupert Sheldrake (infamous, to the more hidebound biologists) summarized Lasley's results as follows:

> He trained rats to learn tricks, then chopped bits of their brains out to determine whether the rats could still do the tricks. To his amazement, he

found that he could remove over 50% of the brain, any 50%, and there would be virtually no effect on the retention of learning.[4]

If anything, Sheldrake understates the situation. As much as 80 percent of the brain can be destroyed and some memory functions still operate.

> At one point a nonplused Lashley said wryly that his research demonstrated that learning was just not possible.[5]
>
> . . . [Lashley] also proposed something that seemed at the time a rather pathetic notion to cover this failure. The engram was there, Lashley ventured, but in some wholly illogical way was spread throughout the entire brain. Moreover, to top off this fogginess, he suggested that memories were formed by the action of something called "interference waves."[6]

As we will see later, there actually is a strange type of photograph, called a hologram, which records "interference patterns," and spreads them throughout the entire surface of the film. It is the most efficient memory storage method ever devised, and nature rarely ignores efficient methods. But before we discuss holograms, we need to take a short detour through the route that led Pribram to his holographic model of the brain. In chapter 3, we briefly followed a history of thought that led from Locke's "blank slate" model of the brain to a "feed-forward" model (which,

---

[4] Rupert Sheldrake, "Mind, Memory and Archetype," in *Psychological Perspectives*, Spring, 1987.

[5] Marilyn Ferguson, "Karl Pribram's Changing Reality," in *Brain/Mind Bulletin*, 1978, p. 16.

[6] David Loye, *The Sphinx and the Rainbow* (New York: Bantam, 1983), p. 186.

incidentally, Pribram championed as an intermediate model before he came to his holographic model). Here we pass beyond "feed-forward" to "holographic."

FROM STIMULUS/RESPONSE TO HOLOGRAPHIC

When Pribram began his career as a neurophysiologist, he considered himself a "staunch behaviorist." Like other behaviorists, he viewed the reflex arc as the elementary model of the operation of the brain. In such a model, a stimulus leads directly to a response with no intervening mental operations. But two key results by fellow scientists convinced Pribram that the reflex arc wasn't a sufficiently complex model.

> Two major experimental results emerged during the 1950's that were difficult to contain in stimulus-response terms. The first of these was the finding . . . that rats with hypothalmic lesions would overeat and become obese in ad libitum feeding situation but would starve if they had to work even slightly for their food . . .
>
> The second major finding was that a large portion of the output fibers from the spinal cord to muscles ended not on contractile tissue but on muscle receptors.[7]

This first finding seemed incompatible with any theory which didn't allow for some degree of intentionality, of "effort." Of course, behavioral science's reflex arc model has no room for such arcane concepts as "effort." The sec-

---

[7] Karl Pribram, "The Brain," in *Millennium: Glimpses into the 21st Century*, edited by A. Villoldo and K. Dychtwald (Los Angeles: J. P. Tarcher, 1981), p. 96.

ond finding showed that the central nervous system (including the brain) is able to send impulses that appear the same to the receptors as sensory input from the outer world. In other words, our senses have no idea whether they are perceiving the outer world, or perceiving a model of the outer world presented to them by the brain.

Therefore, *at a minimum*, the brain has to continually distinguish between information from the inner and outer worlds, so that it knows which is which. *At a minimum*, the brain has to be able to have some way of *representing* its inner state at all points in time. Rather than an outer stimulus leading ineluctably to an inner response, the brain is continually "predicting the required future response in advance of receiving sensory information" (as we said in chapter 3). Behavioral science viewed complex behaviors as merely "tautological" chains of stimulus-response units. These two studies (among many others) showed Pribram that the brain was far more complex.

But there was more to come. As early as the 19th century, there was already evidence that the auditory brain could analyze sound waves. By Pribram's time, there had been further studies which indicated that sight and touch and perhaps even taste were also processed by the brain as wave forms. What made these discoveries so meaningful was the discovery of the hologram which stores information in terms of wave forms. The Hungarian/British physicist Dennis Gabor received the Nobel prize for his 1947 discovery that holographic photography was mathematically feasible. In 1965, the newly invented laser beam was used to actually construct a hologram. Holograms had the intriguing ability to reproduce a solid 3-dimensional image, though recorded on a 2-dimensional piece of film.

Remember the small 3-dimensional views of Princess Leia and Ben Kenobi in the "Star Wars" movies? Princess Leia looked like a miniature human from all angles; that image was a hologram. It's produced by shining light through a film like a normal photograph, yet the light comes out 3-dimensional. Why it does so is what concerns us next.

MAKING A HOLOGRAM

A normal photograph is an straight-forward 2-dimensional copy of the object photographed; it's a more advanced version of hand shadows on the wall. A hologram is very different. Imagine that we want to construct a hologram of some object, say a watch. First we put a very strong, coherent light source (i.e., a laser) at one end of a room and the recording film at the other end. Just in front of the light source, put a prism which splits the beam into two equal beams that go out at 45 degree angles on each side. Place two mirrors such that they each catch one of the light beams and reflect it toward the recording film. Finally take away one of the mirrors and place the watch where the mirror was.

The light which strikes the watch is still reflected and part of it hits the recording film, but it hits it at all sorts of angles depending on the surface of the watch off of which it bounced. If we'd examine the piece of film, it would appear to have a seemingly random pattern of light and dark shapes. That pattern of light and dark is actually the "interference pattern" formed when the two streams of light waves arrived at the film together. Every surfer knows about interference patterns. Waves have peaks and troughs. When the waves roll in, with either their peaks or troughs coinciding, the surfer will have monster waves or "holes" respectively. When the peaks and troughs meet, they cancel each other out and the surfer is stuck with useless choppy waves. Human moods also follow cyclic patterns. If a husband is in a good mood at the same time as his wife, they have a terrific time, much better than either would have alone. When they're both in bad moods, oh my! But most of the time, their moods won't be perfectly aligned; he's more "up" than she is, or vice versa. We all know what a complex pattern that forms in our lives.

Light is also a wave phenomenon; when the light waves hit the film, they form interference patterns where the peaks and troughs coincide or interfere. That interference pattern is what the hologram records. If we shine the light through our holographic film of the watch, an exact three-dimensional image of the watch appears in mid-air, seemingly as solid as the watch. We're unraveling the interference, inferring the original image from the interference pattern.

But here's the real surprise. Cut a piece of the film from the larger piece. We'll pretend that it's only one tenth the size of the full film; we can take it from any part of the film. If we again shine the light through this small piece of film, again we see a full three-dimensional image of the watch! If we cut a piece only one hundredth as big as the original and shine a light through it, the watch will appear still again, though perhaps looking a little fuzzy. If we take a piece only a thousandth the size of the original, a full view will still be seen, but by this time it may be so diffuse that we can hardly make it out. It will look wispy, ghost-like.

We're so used to the way a lens like a camera lens or the lens of our eye focuses a solid image onto a flat surface that it's difficult to understand why a hologram works. There are an enormous number of light waves reflected from the surface of the watch at angles uniquely determined by the shape of the watch, yet concentrated by reflection onto the film. A duplicate beam, usually called the "reference beam," is also arriving at the film at the same time. If we hadn't replaced our original reflecting mirror with the watch, the two beams would arrive together, perfectly synchronized. The peaks of one would match the peak of the other, the troughs of one the troughs of the other. There would be no interference pattern at all.

But, because one light beam first bounced off the irregular surface of the watch, everywhere on the film light waves are interfering in ways that are unique to the image of the watch. When an identical "reference beam" shines through the film, it creates the irregular surface of the watch that created the pattern in the first place. Wherever light hits the film, there is a complex interference pattern created by the total surface of the watch. That's why any portion of the film can reproduce the entire hologram of the watch. The more such interference patterns we have, the better, clearer image we get, but any portion of the film is still uniquely determined by the light waves that bounced off the watch.

THE WORLD AS A HOLOGRAM

... thanks to the prodigious biological event rep- resented by the discovery of electromagnetic waves, each individual finds himself henceforth (actively and passively) simultaneously present, over land and sea, in every corner of the earth.[8]

The hologram was an intensely exciting discovery for scien- tists of many different fields. As a neurophysiologist, Pri- bram naturally tried to adapt this new model of information storage to the nature of the brain; he asked himself if per- haps the brain stores information holographically. If so, we would expect that memory storage should be diffuse throughout the brain. As you will recall, this was exactly the situation Lashley encountered in his futile attempts to local- ize memories. If, as Lashley found, most of the brain can be removed without affecting learning, the brain must be able to store information diffusely.

If the brain is a hologram, then one would expect that sensory perceptions must be received in wave form, since holograms are formed from the interference patterns of waves. And, again as we have already discussed, that is exactly how sense impressions are processed by the body.

---

[8] Marshall McLuhan and Quentin Fiore, *The Medium is the Massage*, p. 32.

This was a marvelous discovery by Pribram, but some time later, he came to a much greater realization: that perhaps the world is itself a hologram! The human brain records sensory information holographically because the universe it records is a hologram. That is, the supposed "objects" that make up our world are really the intersection of waves.

Why should this be so? In fact, all the "forces" (i.e., gravity, light, sound, etc.) and all the supposedly material particles of the universe can be expressed as a wave phenomenon (at least in part). We are all aware of sound waves and light waves, infrared and ultraviolet waves, but we probably aren't all aware that all matter consists of waves. Electrons are waves, neutrons are waves, protons are waves, all particles are waves. (They are also particles, but that's another story.)

If everything in the world is a wave, then everywhere those waves are meeting in gorgeous, abstract patterns throughout all eternity. The whole universe becomes a tapestry, as poets and mystics have told us for centuries. But it remained for Karl Pribram to discover how the world of the poets and the mystics, and the seemingly ordinary world we think we live in, meet in the holographic transformation that occurs in each of our brains.

> . . . If holographic representations within the brain do not exist in terms of the familiar space-time coordinates, then perhaps there are orders of the universe outside that also do not exist in ordinary space-time. . . . This could mean that physical orders exist in which synchronicity rather than causality operates as a basic principle. . . . This could mean that beyond every appearance of randomness lies hidden an order that awaits discovery.[9]

---

[9] Karl Pribram, "The Brain," in *Millennium: Glimpses into the 21st Century*, edited by A. Villoldo and K. Dychtwald, 1981, p. 102.

THE "ALEPH"

God (or nature) is an intelligible (or infinite or
frightful) sphere whose center is everywhere,
whose circumference is no-where."[10]

Let's turn back from Pribram's holographic universe to
Kurt Gödel. In the last chapter, we briefly traced the history
of mathematics which led up to Gödel's remarkable proof
that logic is inherently limited. But I left the core of Gödel's
method for this present chapter. In brief, Gödel took every
"sign" that mathematicians and logicians use in discussing
arithmetic, i.e., their "language," and converted each sign
into a unique number: a "Gödel number."

Since a mathematical equation is nothing but a
sequence of numbers and signs, Gödel could convert an
equation into a sequence of Gödel numbers. He then used a
clever mathematical trick (which need not concern us here)
to convert the sequence of Gödel numbers into a unique
Gödel number. Thus an equation could be represented by a
single number.

Since a mathematical proof is a sequence of mathematical statements (i.e., equations), Gödel could convert a proof
into still another sequence of Gödel numbers, and that
sequence in turn into a single, unique Gödel number. One
number thus stood for a whole mathematical proof! What a
seeming triumph of reductionism.

Now consider that the goal of science—of rationalism
itself—is to make the universe logically intelligible. Science feels that ultimately all of nature can be logically
explained in terms of the quantities and movements of
material bodies. Most of us are aware of the irreparable
damage that the discoveries of modern physics have done

---

[10] Alain de Lille and Pascal, separately, quotation in Jorge Luis Borges,
Other Inquisitions: 1937–1952 (Austin, TX: University of Texas Press,
1968).

to the materialist side of the rationalist/materialist position. There really isn't much matter left in supposedly material bodies after relativity and quantum mechanics. Nuclear physicists today discuss the structure of matter in terms of quarks, and quarks are defined whimsically in terms of properties such as "strangeness," "charm," and "flavor," which have no relationship to anything we normally think of as material.

So rationalism is reduced to a faith in logic, and the capstone of logic is mathematics. The mathematical formalists we traced in the previous chapter felt that reality could be reduced to science, science to mathematics, mathematics to arithmetic. Gödel took this argument to the point of logical absurdity. Gödel showed that an arithmetic proof could be reduced to a single number. By implication, the Gödel numbers of all arithmetic proofs could be further reduced to a single number. In other words, if the goal of the formalists had been correct and reality could be reduced to logic, Gödel's construction method could reduce all of reality to a single number! But, of course, in the process, Gödel demonstrated that logic was insufficient to the task at hand, the universe was too complex to be subsumed under logical analysis.

This is a concept that the great Argentinian writer, Jorge Luis Borges, returned to time and again in his writings. For example, in "The Aleph," he said that the Aleph was the single place in the world where "without any possible confusion, all the places in the world are found, seen from every angle."[11] Gödel's enormous number and Borges' Aleph are like the unutterable name of God: because they contain everything, they are beyond description.

That was Gödel's point: that every number was a mystery containing the whole universe. If this whole concept seems far removed from normal life, consider the Gross National Product (GNP). This is a single number, calculated

---

[11] Jorge Luis Borges, *A Personal Anthology* (New York: Castle Books, 1967), p. 147.

and published every month that purports to measure our country's total productivity, the sum of all its products and services. Obviously, no single number can begin to do any such thing, but the GNP has acquired almost magical status. Economists develop definitions of recession versus depression depending on the number of times the GNP decreases over a given period of time. The GNP is not a number which can be reduced to a single definition, it's the center of a whole panoply of associations; i.e., it's a symbol in the full sense that Jung uses the term.

If a single number can potentially contain the universe, it is only because that number is a symbolic content of the human mind. Each individual human being—like God and the universe—is an "infinite sphere whose center is everywhere, whose circumference is nowhere." It is in that sense that each human being is the center of the universe, that each contains the universe. Similarly for Pribram, the universe is not made up of individual "things"; the universe is an interplay of probabilities (which is another way of saying that it's made up of waves). Consciousness actualizes those possibilities. In that sense, the mind creates the universe. Gödel and Pribram provide new symbols for expressing the seemingly inexpressible nature of the universe. Jolin's vision deals with the same topic.

THE TEMPLE OF GOD—GOD AS TEMPLE

And I saw no temple therein: for the Lord God Almighty and the Lamb are the temple of it. And the city had no need of the sun, neither of the moon, to shine in it: for the glory of God did lighten it, and the Lamb is the light thereof. And the nations of them which are saved shall walk in the light of it: and the kings of the earth do bring

their glory and honour into it. And the gates of it
shall not be shut at all by day, for there shall be no
night there (21:22–25).

The temple was the center of the old Jerusalem; here in the
New Jerusalem the center is God himself! The vision is
stressing that the New Jerusalem is not a place but a state of
being: a state of being where God (i.e., the Self) and
mankind are in balance. In that state of harmony, there is no
need of intermediaries such as religions, priests, temples.
God is the temple and God is accessible within each person.
Similarly, there is no need for external light, external revelation; the light is contained within each of us. A holographic
world indeed!

And he shewed me a pure river of water of life,
clear as crystal, proceeding out of the throne of
God and of the Lamb (22:1).

Once we dwell in this state, we will have a clear, flowing,
organic connection with the God-force within.

In the midst of the street of it, and on either side
of the river, was there the tree of life, which bare
twelve manner of fruits, and yielded her fruit
every month: and the leaves of the tree were for
the healing of the nations. And there shall be no
more curse (22:2–3).

With this mention of the "tree of life" and the "curse," the
Vision brings us back full circle to the beginning of the
Bible, the beginning of the long journey toward conscious-
ness. In Genesis, we are told that:

And the LORD God said, Behold, the man is
become as one of us, to know good and evil: and
now, lest he put forth his hand, and take also of

the tree of life, and eat, and live for ever. Therefore the LORD God sent him forth from the garden of Eden, to till the ground from whence he
was taken. So he drove out the man; and he
placed at the east of the garden of Eden Cheru-
bims, and a flaming sword which turned every
way, to keep the way, of the tree of life (Genesis
3:22–24).

Here mankind has at last found atonement (literally atonement) for temerity in the Garden. Now the leaves of the
tree will heal our wounds, now the tree itself grows inside
mankind and "there shall be no more curse." What would
such a world be like? Can we even begin to comprehend it?
At the risk of seeming ridiculously presumptuous, let me
begin an attempt at a description of what that all means in
human terms. I've pictured the era just ending—the Christian era—as the era of the god/human: the era when we
first began to realize that the divine might be located
within, not without.

Jehovah was a god of stern retribution: "An eye for an
eye." In contrast, Christ's message was "love thy neighbor
as thyself." As the Gnostics and later the Sufis understood,
the esoteric underpinning of that message was "love your
neighbor as you love yourself, because he is yourself." Similarly, five centuries earlier, Buddha taught the Eastern
world how to escape from the delusion that we can be
defined by any of our attributes—physical appearance,
occupation, morality, creativity, etc. For Buddha, after all
such ephemera are stripped away, the essential Self
remains. Mankind had already realized that God could not
be delimited by any qualities attributed to us; we now
made that discovery about ourselves.

The "membrane" that separates individual humans
from their total environment is highly permeable; i.e., where
do you and I end and the universe begin? Dismissing such
an experience as delusional is highly suspect because of its

repeatability, especially its repeatability among a wide variety of people in a wide variety of cultures using a wide variety of techniques. This transcendent experience seems to be inherent in the combined (or perhaps unitary) structure of human beings and the universe in which they live. Though the day-to-day world doesn't readily yield to transcendence, if you or I are feeling good about ourselves, other people feel better when they come into contact with us. And there has been behavioral research which demonstrates that a simple human touch makes us feel better (even if the touch is not noticed: such as the brush of a bank cashier's hand in giving us our change).

Jung loved to repeat a story about a Chinese rainmaker which his friend Richard Wilhelm, the translator of the *I Ching* and *The Secret of the Golden Flower*, told him was a personal experience. Wilhelm was visiting a village devastated by a drought at a time when they sent for a rainmaker. When the rainmaker—who, as was normal in China at the time, was a Buddhist priest—arrived, he was asked what he would require. He asked only for a small hut to live in at the edge of the village. He then retired to that hut.

At the end of three days, he came out of the hut and it began to rain. While the people of the village scampered in delight, Wilhelm asked the priest how he had brought the rain. The priest said that when he came to the village, he could feel that it was "out of Tao"; that is, emotionally disturbed. That made him feel "out of Tao" as well. So he withdrew to the hut until he was once more "in Tao." When he did so, the rain came.

The goal is to experience life simultaneously as both a personal experience and a symbolic act. This is hard to describe, but it can become normal to look at every action in the day, every person we come into contact with, every event we hear about in the world as symbolic. Outer events seem to speak to our inner needs. Personal experience seems to speak to outer events. Our lives seem synchronous with those around us, for better or worse.

Once this becomes as normal as waking and working and playing and sleeping, it ceases to be the amazing thing it seems in the early stages of self-realization. One's unity with others and with the universe seems self-evident, not merely intellectually self-evident, but experientially. While living life in this dual manner doesn't eliminate life's normal problems, it raises them to mythic proportion which—unexpectedly enough—frequently makes them vanish. After all, once you realize that a problem is a global problem, not some personal problem you can easily resolve, it is difficult to stay lost in guilt and self-recrimination. As I've argued throughout this book, we are living through what I believe to be humanity's major transition of consciousness. The problems humanity faces at this watershed in history are enormous. The concomitant strains on each individual—especially to the extent that the individual consciously participates in this transitional struggle—are equally enormous.

On this note, we come to an end of our exploration of John's magnificent vision. The angel told John at the end of the vision: "Seal not the sayings of the prophecy of this book; for the time is at hand." That has been my purpose in writing so much about the Book of Revelation, because I also feel that "the time is at hand." Yet even this exploration covers only a tiny part of the wisdom of the vision. We can each learn to open the doors of our hearts a little wider and peek into the New Jerusalem. "The Spirit and the Bride say: Come."

APPENDIX

THE REVELATION OF ST. JOHN THE DIVINE

Figure 29. All great visions come from individuals who are willing to separate themselves from the crowd, and look within. Strangely enough, that process leads to the discovery of a new "living symbol" which can speak to all humanity. ("St. John at Patmos," Gustave Doré, first published in *La Sainte Bible*, 1860.)

APPENDIX

THE REVELATION OF ST. JOHN THE DIVINE

CHAPTER 1

1   The Revelation of Jesus Christ, which God gave unto him, to shew unto his servants things which must shortly come to pass; and he sent and signified it by his angel unto his servant John:

2   Who bare record of the word of God, and of the testimony of Jesus Christ, and of all things that he saw.

3   Blessed is he that readeth, and they that hear the words of this prophecy, and keep those things which are written therein; for the time is at hand.

4   John to the seven churches which are in Asia: Grace be unto you, and peace, from him which is, and which was, and which is to come; and from the seven Spirits which are before his throne;

5   And from Jesus Christ, who is the faithful witness, and the first begotten of the dead, and the prince of the kings of the earth. Unto him that loved us, and washed us from our sins in his own blood,

6   And hath made us kings and priests unto God and his Father; to him be glory and dominion for ever and ever. Amen.

7   Behold, he cometh with clouds; and every eye shall see him, and they also which pierced him: and all kindreds of the earth shall wail because of him. Even so, Amen.

8   I am Alpha and Omega, the beginning and the ending, saith the Lord, which is, and which was, and which is to come, the Almighty.

9   I John, who also am your brother, and companion in tribulation, and in the kingdom and patience of Jesus Christ, was in the isle that is called Patmos, for the word of God, and for the testimony of Jesus Christ.

10   I was in the Spirit on the Lord's day, and heard behind me a great voice, as of a trumpet,

11   Saying, I am Alpha and Omega, the first and the last: and, What thou seest, write in a book, and send it unto the seven churches which are in Asia; unto Ephesus, and unto Smyrna, and unto Pergamos, and unto Thyatira, and unto Sardis, and unto Philadelphia, and unto Laodicea.

12 And I turned to see the voice that spake with me. And being turned, I saw seven golden candlesticks;

13 And in the midst of the seven candlesticks one like unto the Son of man, clothed with a garment down to the foot, and girt about the paps with a golden girdle.

14 His head and his hairs were white like wool, as white as snow; and his eyes were as a flame of fire;

15 And his feet like unto fine brass, as if they burned in a furnace; and his voice as the sound of many waters.

16 And he had in his right hand seven stars: and out of his mouth went a sharp twoedged sword; and his countenance was as the sun shineth in his strength.

17 And when I saw him, I fell at his feet as dead. And he laid his right hand upon me, saying unto me, Fear not; I am the first and the last;

18 I am he that liveth, and was dead; and, behold, I am alive for evermore, Amen; and have the keys of hell and of death.

19 Write the things which thou hast seen, and the things which are, and the things which shall be hereafter;

20 The mystery of the seven stars which thou sawest in my right hand, and the seven golden candlesticks. The seven stars are the angels of the seven churches; and the seven candlesticks which thou sawest are the seven churches.

CHAPTER 2

1 Unto the angel of the church of Ephesus write; These things saith he that holdeth the seven stars in his right hand, who walketh in the midst of the seven golden candlesticks;

2 I know thy works, and thy labour, and thy patience, and how thou canst not bear them which are evil: and thou hast tried them which say they are apostles and are not, and has found them liars:

3 And hast borne, and has patience, and for my name's sake has laboured, and hast not fainted.

4 Nevertheless I have somewhat against thee, because thou hast left thy first love.

5 Remember therefore from whence thou art fallen, and repent, and do the first works; or else I will come unto thee quickly, an will remove they candlestick out of his place, except thou repent.

6 But this thou hast, that thou hatest the deeds of the Nicolaitanes, which I also hate.

7 He that hath an ear, let him hear what the Spirit saith unto the churches; To him that overcometh will I give to eat of the tree of life, which is in the midst of the paradise of God.

8   And unto the angel of the church in Smyrna write; These things saith the first and the last, which was dead, and is alive;

9   I know thy works, and tribulation, and poverty, (but thou art rich) and I know the blasphemy of them which say they are Jews, and are not, but are the synagogue of Satan.

10   Fear none of those things which thou shalt suffer: behold, the devil shall cast some of you into prison, that ye may be tried; and ye shall have tribulation ten days: be thou faithful unto death, and I will give thee a crown of life.

11   He that hath an ear, let him hear what the Spirit saith unto the churches; He that overcometh shall not be hurt of the second death.

12   And to the angel of the church in Pergamos write; These things saith he which hath the sharp sword with two edges;

13   I know thy works, and where thou dwellest, even where Satan's seat is: and thou holdest fast my name, and has not denied my faith, even in those days wherein Antipas was my faithful martyr, who was slain among you, where Satan dwelleth.

14   But I have a few things against thee, because thou hast there them that hold the doctrine of Balaam, who taught Balac to cast a stumbling block before the children of Israel, to eat things sacrificed unto idols, and to commit fornication.

15   So hast thou also them that hold the doctrine of Nicolaitanes, which thing I hate.

16   Repent; or else I will come unto thee quickly, and will fight against them with the sword of my mouth.

17   He that hath an ear, let him hear what the Spirit saith unto the churches; To him that overcometh will I give to eat of the hidden manna, and will give him a white stone, and in the stone a new name written, which no man knoweth saving he that receiveth it.

18   And unto the angel of the church in Thyatira write; These things saith the Son of God, who hath his eyes like unto a flame of fire, and his feet are like fine brass;

19   I know thy works, and charity, and service, and faith, and thy patience, and thy works; and the last to be more than the first.

20   Notwithstanding I have a few things against thee, because thou sufferest that woman Jezebel, which calleth herself a prophetess, to teach and to seduce my servants to commit fornication, and to eat things sacrificed unto idols.

21   And I gave her space to repent of her fornication, and she repented not.

22   Behold, I will cast her into a bed, and them that commit adultery with her into great tribulation, except they repent of their deeds.

23   And I will kill her children with death; and all the churches shall know that I am he which searcheth the reins and hearts: and I will give unto every one of you according to your works.

24   But unto you I say, and unto the rest in Thyatira, as many as have not this doctrine, and which have not known the depths of Satan, as they speak; I will put upon you none other burden.
25   But that which ye have already hold fast till I come.
26   And he that overcometh, and keepeth my works unto the end, to him will I give power over the nations:
27   And he shall rule them with a rod of iron; as the vessels of a potter shall they be broken to shivers: even as I received of my Father.
28   And I will give him the morning star.
29   He that hath an ear, let him hear what the Spirit saith unto the churches.

CHAPTER 3

1   And unto the angel of the church in Sardis write; These things saith he that hath the seven Spirits of God, and the seven stars; I know thy works, that thou hast a name that thou livest, and art dead.
2   Be watchful, and strengthen the things which remain that are ready to die: for I have not found thy works perfect before God.
3   Remember therefore how thou has received and heard, and hold fast, and repent. If therefore thou shalt not watch, I will come on thee as a thief, and thou shalt not know what hour I will come upon thee.
4   Thou hast a few names even in Sardis which have not defiled their garments; and they shall walk with me in white: for they are worthy.
5   He that overcometh, the same shall be clothed in white raiment; and I will not blot out his name out of the book of life, but I will confess his name before my Father, and before his angels.
6   He that hath an ear, let him hear what the Spirit saith unto the churches.
7   And to the angel of the church in Philadelphia write; These things saith he that is holy, he that is true, he that hath the key of David, he that openeth, and no man shutteth; and shutteth, and no man openeth;
8   I know thy works: behold, I have set before thee an open door, and no man can shut it; for thou hast a little strength, and has kept my word, and hast not denied my name.
9   Behold, I will make them of the synagogue of Satan, which say they are Jews, and are not, but do lie; behold, I will make them to come and worship before thy feet, and to know that I have loved thee.
10   Because thou hast kept the word of my patience, I also will keep thee from the hour of temptation, which shall come upon all the world, to try them that dwell upon the earth.
11   Behold, I come quickly: hold that fast which thou hast, that no man take thy crown.

12   Him that overcometh will I make a pillar in the temple of my God, and he shall go no more out: and I will write upon him the name of my God, and the name of the city of my God, which is new Jerusalem, which cometh down out of heaven from my God: and I will write upon him my new name.

13   He that hath an ear, let him hear what the Spirit saith unto the churches.

14   And unto the angel of the church of the Laodiceans write; These things saith the Amen, the faithful and true witness, the beginning of the creation of God;

15   I know thy works, that thou art neither cold nor hot: I would thou wert cold or hot.

16   So then because thou art lukewarm, and neither cold nor hot, I will spue thee out of my mouth.

17   Because thou sayest, I am rich, and increased with goods, and have need of nothing; and knowest not that thou art wretched, and miserable, and poor, and blind, and naked:

18   I counsel thee to buy of me gold tried in the fire, that thou mayest be rich; and white raiment, that thou mayest be clothed, and that the shame of thy nakedness do not appear; and anoint thine eyes with eyesalve, that thou mayest see.

19   As many as I love, I rebuke and chasten: be zealous therefore, and repent.

20   Behold, I stand at the door, and knock: if any man hear my voice, and open the door, I will come in to him, and will sup with him, and he with me.

21   To him that overcometh will I grant to sit with me in my throne, even as I also overcame, and am set down with my Father in his throne.

22   He that hath an ear, let him hear what the Spirit saith unto the churches.

CHAPTER 4

1   After this I looked, and, behold, a door was opened in heaven: and the first voice which I heard was as it were of a trumpet talking with me; which said, Come up hither, and I will shew thee things which must be hereafter.

2   And immediately I was in the spirit: and, behold, a throne was set in heaven, and one sat on the throne.

3   And he that sat was to look upon like a jasper and a sardine stone: and there was a rainbow round about the throne, in sight like unto an emerald.

4   And round about the throne were four and twenty seats: and upon the seats I saw four and twenty elders sitting, clothed in white raiment; and they had on their heads crowns of gold.

5   And out of the throne proceeded lightnings and thunderings and voices: and there were seven lamps of fire burning before the throne, which are the seven Spirits of God.

6   And before the throne there was a sea of glass like unto crystal: and in the midst of the throne, and round about the throne, were four beasts full of eyes before and behind.

7   And the first beast was like a lion, and the second beast like a calf, and the third beast had a face as a man, and the fourth beast was like a flying eagle.

8   And the four beasts had each of them six wings about him and they were full of eyes within: and they rest not day and night, saying, Holy, holy, holy, Lord God Almighty, which was, and is, and is to come.

9   And when those beasts give glory and honour and thanks to him that sat on the throne, who liveth for ever and ever,

10   The four and twenty elders fall down before him that sat on the throne, and worship him that liveth for ever and ever, and cast their crowns before the throne, saying,

11   Thou art worthy, O Lord, to receive glory and honour and power: for thou hast created all things, and for thy pleasure they are and were created.

CHAPTER 5

1   And I saw in the right hand of him that sat on the throne a book written within and on the backside, sealed with seven seals.

2   And I saw a strong angel proclaiming with a loud voice, Who is worthy to open the book, and to loose the seals thereof?

3   And no man in heaven, nor in earth, neither under the earth, was able to open the book, neither to look thereon.

4   And I wept much, because no man was found worthy to open and to read the book, neither to look thereon.

5   And one of the elders saith unto me, Weep not: behold, the Lion of the tribe of Juda, the Root of David, hath prevailed to open the book, and to loose the seven seals thereof.

6   And I beheld, and, lo, in the midst of the throne and of the four beasts, and in the midst of the elders, stood a Lamb as it had been slain, having seven horns and seven eyes, which are the seven Spirits of God sent forth into all the earth.

7   And he came and took the book out of the right hand of him that sat upon the throne.

8   And when he had taken the book, the four beasts and four and twenty elders fell down before the Lamb, having every one of them harps, and golden vials full of odours, which are the prayers of saints.

9   And they sung a new song, saying, Thou are worthy to take the book, and to open the seals thereof: for thou wast slain, and hast redeemed us to God by thy blood out of every kindred, and tongue, and people, and nation;

10   And hast made us unto our God kings and priests: and we shall reign on the earth.

11   And I beheld, and I heard the voice of many angels round about the throne and the beasts and the elders: and the number of them was ten thousand times ten thousand, and thousands of thousands;

12   Saying with a loud voice, Worthy is the Lamb that was slain to receive power, and riches, and wisdom, and strength, and honour, and glory, and blessing.

13   And every creature which is in heaven, and on the earth, and under the earth, and such as are in the sea, and all that are in them, heard I saying, Blessing, and honour, and glory, and power, be unto him that sitteth upon the throne, and unto the Lamb for ever and ever.

14   And the four beasts said, Amen. And the four and twenty elders fell down and worshiped him that liveth for ever and ever.

CHAPTER 6

1   And I saw when the Lamb opened one of the seals, and I heard, as it were the noise of thunder, one of the four beasts saying, Come and see.

2   And I saw, and behold a white horse: and he that sat on him had a bow; and a crown was given unto him: and he went forth conquering, and to conquer.

3   And when he had opened the second seal, I heard the second beast say, Come and see.

4   And there went out another horse that was red: and power was given to him that sat thereon to take peace from the earth, and that they should kill one another: and there was given unto him a great sword.

5   And when he had opened the third seal, I heard the third beast say, Come and see. And I beheld, and lo a black horse; and he that sat on him had a pair of balances in his hand.

6   And I heard a voice in the midst of the four beasts say, A measure of wheat for a penny, and three measures of barley for a penny; and see thou hurt not the oil and the wine.

7   And when he had opened the fourth seal, I heard the voice of the fourth beast say, Come and see.

8   And I looked, and behold a pale horse: and his name that sat on him was death, and Hell followed with him. And power was given unto them over the fourth part of the earth, to kill with sword, and with hunger, and with death, and with the beasts of the earth.

9   And when he had opened the fifth seal, I saw under the altar the souls of them that were slain for the word of God, and for the testimony which they held:

10   And they cried with a loud voice, saying, How long, O Lord, holy and true, dost thou not judge and avenge our blood on them that dwell on the earth?

11   And white robes were given unto every one of them; and it was said unto them, that they should rest yet for a little season, until their fellow-servants also and their brethren, that should be killed as they were, should be fulfilled.

12   And I beheld when he had opened the sixth seal, and, lo, there was a great earthquake; and thy sun became black as sackcloth of hair, and the moon became as blood;

13   And the stars of heaven fell unto the earth, even as a fig tree casteth her untimely figs, when she is shaken of a mighty wind.

14   And the heaven departed as a scroll when it is rolled together; and every mountain and island were moved out of their places.

15   And the kings of the earth, and the great men, and the rich men, and the chief captains, and the mighty men, and every bondman, and every free man, hid themselves in the dens and in the rocks of the mountains.

16   And said to the mountains and rocks, Fall on us, and hide us from the face of him that sitteth on the throne, and from the wrath of the Lamb:

17   For the great day of his wrath is come; and who shall be able to stand?

CHAPTER 7

1   And after these things I saw four angels standing on the four corners of the earth, holding the four winds of the earth, that the wind should not blow on the earth, nor on the sea, nor on any tree.

2   And I saw another angel ascending from the east, having the seal of the living God: and he cried with a loud voice to the four angels, to whom it was given to hurt the earth and the sea,

3   Saying, Hurt not the earth, neither the sea, nor the trees, till we have sealed the servants of our God in their foreheads.

4   And I heard the number of them which were sealed: and there were sealed an hundred and forty and four thousand of all the tribes of the children of Israel.

5   Of the tribe of Juda were sealed twelve thousand. Of the tribe of Reuben were sealed twelve thousand. Of the tribe of Gad were sealed twelve thousand.

6   Of the tribe of Aser were sealed twelve thousand. Of the tribe of Nepthalim were sealed twelve thousand. Of the tribe of Manasses were sealed twelve thousand.

7   Of the tribe of Simeon were sealed twelve thousand. Of the tribe of Levi were sealed twelve thousand. Of the tribe of Issachar were sealed twelve thousand.

8   Of the tribe of Zabulon were sealed twelve thousand. Of the tribe of Joseph were sealed twelve thousand. Of the tribe of Benjamin were sealed twelve thousand.

9   After this I beheld, and, lo, a great multitude, which no man could number, of all nations, and kindreds, and people, and tongues, stood before the throne, and before the Lamb, clothed with white robes, and palms in their hands;

10   And cried with a loud voice, saying, Salvation to our God which sitteth upon the throne, and unto the Lamb.

11   And all the angels stood round about the throne, and about the elders and the four beasts, and fell before the throne on their faces, and worshiped God,

12   Saying, Amen: Blessing, and glory, and wisdom, and thanksgiving, and honour, and power, and might, be unto our God for ever and ever. Amen.

13   And one of the elders answered, saying unto me, What are these which are arrayed in white robes? and whence came they?

14   And I said unto him, Sir, thou knowest. And he said to me, These are they which came out of great tribulation, and have washed their robes, and made them white in the blood of the Lamb.

15   Therefore are they before the throne of God, and serve him day and night in his temple: and he that sitteth on the throne shall dwell among them.

16   They shall hunger no more, neither thirst any more; neither shall the sun light on them, nor any heat.

17   For the Lamb which is in the midst of the throne shall feed them, and shall lead them unto living fountains of waters: and God shall wipe away all tears from their eyes.

CHAPTER 8

1   And when he had opened the seventh seal, there was silence in heaven about the space of half an hour.

2   And I saw the seven angels which stood before God; and to them were given seven trumpets.

3   And another angel came and stood at the altar, having a golden censer; and there was given unto him much incense, that he should offer it with the prayers of all saints upon the golden altar which was before the throne.

4   And the smoke of the incense which came with the prayers of the saints, ascended up before God out of the angel's hand.

5   And the angel took the censer, and filled it with fire of the altar, and cast it into the earth: and there were voices, and thunderings, and lightnings, and an earthquake.

6   And the seven angels which had the seven trumpets prepared themselves to sound.

7   The first angel sounded, and there followed hail and fire mingled with blood, and they were cast upon the earth: and the third part of trees was burnt up, and all green grass was burnt up.

8   And the second angel sounded, and as it were a great mountain burning with fire was cast into the sea: and the third part of the sea became blood;

9   And the third part of the creatures which were in the sea, and had life, died; and the third part of the ships were destroyed.

10   And the third angel sounded, and there fell a great star from heaven, burning as it were a lamp, and it fell upon the third part of the rivers, and upon the fountains of waters;

11   And the name of the star is called Wormwood: and the third part of the waters became wormwood; and many men died of the waters, because they were made bitter.

12   And the fourth angel sounded, and the third part of the sun was smitten, and the third part of the moon, and the third part of the stars; so as the third part of them was darkened, and the day shone not for a third part of it, and the night likewise.

13   And I beheld, and heard an angel flying through the midst of heaven, saying with a loud voice, Woe, woe, woe, to the inhabiters of the earth by reason of the other voices of the trumpet of the three angels, which are yet to sound!

CHAPTER 9

1   And the fifth angel sounded, and I saw a star fall from heaven unto earth: and to him was given the key of the bottomless pit.

2   And he opened the bottomless pit; and there arose a smoke out of the pit, as the smoke of a great furnace; and the sun and the air were darkened by reason of the smoke of the pit.

3   And there came out of the smoke locusts upon the earth: and unto them was given power, as the scorpions of the earth have power.

4   And it was commanded them that they should not hurt the grass of the earth, neither any green thing, neither any tree; but only those men which have not the seal of God in their foreheads.

5   And to them it was given that they should not kill them, but that they should be tormented five months: and their torment was as the torment of a scorpion, when he striketh a man.

6   And in those days shall men seek death, and shall not find it; and shall desire to die, and death shall flee from them.

7   And the shapes of the locusts were like unto horses prepared unto battle; and on their heads were as it were crowns like gold, and their faces were as the faces of men.

8   And they had hair as the hair of women, and their teeth were as the teeth of lions.

9   And they had breastplates, as it were breastplates of iron; and the sound of their wings was as the sound of chariots of many horses running to battle.

10   And they had tails like unto scorpions, and there were stings in their tails: and their power was to hurt men five months.

11   And they had a king over them, which is the angel of the bottomless pit, whose name in the Hebrew tongue is Abaddon, but in the Greek tongue hath his name Apollyon.

12   One woe is past; and, behold, there come two woes more hereafter.

13   And the sixth angel sounded, and I heard a voice from the four horns of the golden altar which is before God,

14   Saying to the sixth angel which had the trumpet, Loose the four angels which are bound in the great river Euphrates.

15   And the four angels were loosed, which were prepared for an hour, and a day, and a month, and a year, for to slay the third part of men.

16   And the number of the army of the horsemen were two hundred thousand thousand: and I heard the number of them.

17   And thus I saw the horses in the vision, and them that sat on them, having breastplates of fire, and of jacinth, and brimstone: and the heads of the horses were as the heads of lions; and out of their mouths issued fire and smoke and brimstone.

18   By these three was the third part of men killed, by the fire, and by the smoke, and by the brimstone, which issued out of their mouths.

19   For their power is in their mouth, and in their tails: for their tails were like unto serpents, and had heads, and with them they do hurt.

20   And the rest of the men which were not killed by these plagues yet repented not of the works of their hands, that they should not worship devils, and idols of gold, and silver, and brass, and stone, and of wood: which neither can see, nor hear, nor walk:

21   Neither repented they of their murders, nor of their sorceries, nor of their fornication, nor of their thefts.

CHAPTER 10

1   And I saw another mighty angel come down from heaven, clothed with a cloud: and a rainbow was upon his head, and his face was as it were the sun, and his feet as pillars of fire:

2   And he had in his hand a little book open: and he set his right foot upon the sea, and his left foot on the earth,

3   And cried with a loud voice, as when a lion roareth: and when he had cried, seven thunders uttered their voices.

4   And when the seven thunders had uttered their voices, I was about to write: and I heard a voice from heaven saying unto me, Seal up those things which the seven thunders uttered, and write them not.

5   And the angel which I saw stand upon the sea and upon the earth lifted up his hand to heaven,

6   And sware by him that liveth for ever and ever, who created heaven, and the things that therein are, and the earth, and the things that therein are, and the sea, and the things which are therein, that there should be time no longer.

7   But in the days of the voice of the seventh angel, when he shall begin to sound, the mystery of God should be finished, as he hath declared to his servants the prophets.

8   And the voice which I heard from heaven spake unto me again, and said, Go and take the little book which is open in the hand of the angel which standeth upon the sea and upon the earth.

9   And I went unto the angel, and said unto him, Give me the little book. And he said unto me, Take it, and eat it up; and it shall make thy belly bitter, but it shall be in thy mouth sweet as honey.

10   And I took the little book out of the angel's hand, and ate it up; and it was in my mouth sweet as honey: and as soon as I had eaten it, my belly was bitter.

11   And he said unto me, Thou must prophesy again before many peoples, and nations, and tongues, and kings.

CHAPTER 11

1   And there was given me a reed like unto a rod: and the angel stood, saying, Rise, and measure the temple of God, and the altar, and them that worship therein.

2   But the court which is without the temple leave out, and measure it not; for it is given unto the Gentiles: and the holy city shall they tread under foot forty and two months.

3   And I will give power unto my two witnesses, and they shall prophesy a thousand two hundred and threescore days, clothed in sackcloth.

4   These are the two olive trees, and the two candlesticks standing before the God of the earth.

5   And if any man will hurt them, fire proceedeth out of their mouth, and devoureth their enemies: and if any man will hurt them, he must in this manner be killed.

6   These have power to shut heaven, that it rain not in the days of their prophecy: and have power over waters to turn them to blood, and to smite the earth with all plagues, as often as they will.

7   And when they shall have finished their testimony, the beast that ascendeth out of the bottomless pit shall make war against them, and shall overcome them, and kill them.

8   And their dead bodies shall lie in the street of the great city, which spiritually is called Sodom and Egypt, where also our Lord was crucified.

9   And they of the people and kindreds and tongues and nations shall see their dead bodies three days and an half, and shall not suffer their dead bodies to be put in graves.

10   And they that dwell upon the earth shall rejoice over them, and make merry, and shall send gifts one to another; because these two prophets tormented them that dwelt on the earth.

11   And after three days and an half the Spirit of life from God entered into them, and they stood upon their feet; and great fear fell upon them which saw them.

12   And they heard a great voice from heaven saying unto them, Come up hither. And they ascended up to heaven in a cloud; and their enemies beheld them.

13   And the same hour was there a great earthquake, and the tenth part of the city fell, and in the earthquake were slain of men seven thousand: and the remnant were affrighted, and gave glory to the God of heaven.

14   The second woe is past; and, behold, the third woe cometh quickly.

15   And the seventh angel sounded; and there were great voices in heaven, saying, The kingdoms of this world are become the kingdoms of our Lord, and of his Christ; and he shall reign for ever and ever.

16   And the four and twenty elders, which sat before God on their seats, fell upon their faces, and worshipped God.

17   Saying, We give thee thanks, O Lord God Almighty, which art, and wast, and art to come; because thou hast taken to thee they great power, and hast reigned.

18   And the nations were angry, and thy wrath is come, and the time of the dead, that they should be judged, and that thou shouldest give reward unto thy servants the prophets, and to the saints, and them that fear thy name, small and great; and shouldest destroy them which destroy the earth.

19   And the temple of God was opened in heaven, and there was seen in his temple the ark of his testament: and there were lightnings, and voices, and thunderings, and an earthquake, and great hail.

CHAPTER 12

1   And there appeared a great wonder in heaven; a woman clothed with the sun, and the moon under her feet, and upon her head a crown of twelve stars:

2   And she being with child cried, travailing in birth, and pained to be delivered.

3   And there appeared another wonder in heaven; and behold a great red dragon, having seven heads and ten horns, and seven crowns upon his heads.

4   And his tail drew the third part of the stars of heaven, and did cast them to the earth: and the dragon stood before the woman which was ready to be delivered, for to devour her child as soon as it was born.

5   And she brought forth a man child, who was to rule all nations with a rod of iron: and her child was caught up unto God, and to his throne.

6   And the woman fled into the wilderness, where she hath a place prepared of God, that they should feed her there a thousand two hundred and threescore days.

7   And there was war in heaven: Michael and his angels fought against the dragon; and the dragon fought and his angels,

8   And prevailed not; neither was their place found any more in heaven.

9   And the great dragon was cast out, that old serpent, called the Devil, and Satan, which deceiveth the whole world: he was cast out into the earth, and his angels were cast out with him.

10   And I heard a loud voice saying in heaven, Now is come salvation, and strength, and the kingdom of our God, and the power of his Christ: for the accuser of our brethren is cast down, which accused them before our God day and night.

11   And they overcame him by the blood of the Lamb, and by the word of their testimony; and they loves not their lives unto the death.

12   Therefore rejoice, ye heavens, and ye that dwell in them. Woe to the inhabiters of the earth and of the sea! for the devil is come down unto you, having great wrath, because he knoweth that he hath but a short time.

13   And when the dragon saw that he was cast unto the earth, he perse-
cuted the woman which brought forth the man child.

14   And to the woman were given two wings of a great eagle, that she
might fly into the wilderness, into her place, where she is nourished for a
time, and times, and half a time, from the face of the serpent.

15   And the serpent cast out of his mouth water as a flood after the
woman, that he might cause her to be carried away of the flood.

16   And the earth helped the woman, and the earth opened her mouth,
and swallowed up the flood which the dragon cast out of his mouth.

17   And the dragon was wroth with the woman, and went to make war
with the remnant of her seed, which keep the commandments of God,
and have the testimony of Jesus Christ.

CHAPTER 13

1   And I stood upon the sand of the sea, and saw a beast rise up out of
the sea, having seven heads and ten horns, and upon his horns ten
crowns, and upon his heads the name of blasphemy.

2   And the beast which I saw was like unto a leopard, and his feet were
as the feet of a bear, and his mouth as the mouth of a lion: and the dragon
gave him his power, and his seat, and great authority.

3   And I saw one of his heads as it were wounded to death; and his
deadly wound was healed: and all the world wondered after the beast.

4   And they worshiped the dragon which gave power unto the beast:
and they worshiped the beast, saying, Who is like unto the beast? who is
able to make war with him?

5   And there was given unto him a mouth speaking great things and
blasphemies; and power was given unto him to continue forty and two
months.

6   And he opened his mouth in blasphemy against God, to blaspheme
his name, and his tabernacle, and them that dwell in heaven.

7   And it was given unto him to make war with the saints, and to overcome them: and power was given him over all kindreds, and tongues,
and nations.

8   And all that dwell upon the earth shall worship him, whose names
are not written in the book of life of the Lamb slain from the foundation
of the world.

9   If any man have an ear, let him hear.

10   He that leadeth into captivity shall go into captivity: he that killeth
with the sword must be killed with the sword. Here is the patience and
the faith of the saints.

11   And I beheld another beast coming up out of the earth; and he had
two horns like a lamb, and he spake as a dragon.

12 And he exerciseth all the power of the first beast before him, and causeth the earth and them which dwell therein to worship the first beast, whose deadly wound was healed.

13 And he doeth great wonders, so that he maketh fire come down from heaven on the earth in the sight of men,

14 And deceiveth them that dwell on the earth by the means of those miracles which he had power to do in the sight of the beast; saying to them that dwell on the earth, that they should make an image to the beast, which had the wound by a sword, and did live.

15 And he had power to give life unto the image of the beast, that the image of the beast should both speak, and cause that as many as would not worship the image of the beast should be killed.

16 And he causeth all, both small and great, rich and poor, free and bond, to receive a mark in their right hand, or in their foreheads:

17 And that no man might buy or sell, save he that had the mark, or the name of the beast, or the number of his name.

18 Here is wisdom. Let him that hath understanding count the number of the beast: for it is the number of a man; and his number is Six hundred threescore and six.

CHAPTER 14

1 And I looked, and, lo, a Lamb stood on the mount Sion, and with him an hundred forty and four thousand, having his Father's name written in their foreheads.

2 And I heard a voice from heaven, as the voice of many waters, and as the voice of a great thunder: and I heard the voice of harpers harping with their harps:

3 And they sung as it were a new song before the throne, and before the four beasts, and the elders: and no man could learn that song but the hundred and forty and four thousand, which were redeemed from the earth.

4 These are they which were not defiled with women; for they are virgins. These are they which follow the Lamb whithersoever he goeth. These were redeemed from among men, being the firstfruits unto God and to the Lamb.

5 And in their mouth was found no guile: for they are without fault before the throne of God.

6 And I saw another angel fly in the midst of heaven, having the everlasting gospel to preach unto them that dwell on the earth, and to every nation, and kindred, and tongue, and people.

7 Saying with a loud voice, Fear God, and give glory to him; for the hour of his judgment is come: and worship him that made heaven, and earth, and the sea, and the fountains of waters.

8   And there followed another angel, saying, Babylon is fallen, is fallen, that great city, because she made all nations drink of the wine of the wrath of her fornication.

9   And the third angel followed them, saying with a loud voice, If any man worship the beast and his image, and receive his mark in his forehead, or in his hand,

10   The same shall drink of the wine of the wrath of God, which is poured out without mixture into the cup of his indignation; and he shall be tormented with fire and brimstone in the presence of the holy angels, and in the presence of the Lamb:

11   And the smoke of their torment ascendeth up for ever and ever: and they have no rest day nor night, who worship the beast and his image, and whosoever receiveth the mark of his name.

12   Here is the patience of the saints: here are they that keep the commandments of God, and the faith of Jesus.

13   And I heard a voice from heaven saying unto me, Write, Blessed are the dead which die in the Lord from henceforth: Yea, saith the Spirit, that they may rest from their labours; and their works do follow them.

14   And I looked, and behold a white cloud, and upon the cloud one sat like unto the Son of man, having on his head a golden crown, and in his hand a sharp sickle.

15   And another angel came out of the temple, crying with a loud voice to him that sat on the cloud, Thrust in thy sickle, and reap: for the time is come for thee to reap; for the harvest of the earth is ripe.

16   And he that sat on the cloud thrust in his sickle on the earth; and the earth was reaped.

17   And another angel came out of the temple which is in heaven, he also having a sharp sickle.

18   And another angel came out from the altar, which had power over fire; and cried with a loud cry to him that had the sharp sickle, saying, Thrust in thy sharp sickle, and gather the clusters of the vine of the earth; for her grapes are fully ripe.

19   And the angel thrust in his sickle into the earth, and gathered the vine of the earth, and cast it into the great winepress of the wrath of God.

20   And the winepress was trodden without the city, and blood came out of the winepress, even unto the horse bridles, by the space of a thousand and six hundred furlongs.

CHAPTER 15

1   And I saw another sign in heaven, great and marvellous, seven angels having the seven last plagues; for in them is filled up the wrath of God.

2   And I saw as it were a sea of glass mingled with fire: and them that had gotten the victory over the beast, and over his image, and over his mark, and over the number of his name, stand on the sea of glass, having the harps of God.

3   And they sing the song of Moses the servant of God, and the song of the Lamb, saying, Great and marvellous are thy works, Lord God Almighty; just and true are thy ways, thou King of saints.

4   Who shall not fear thee, O Lord, and glorify thy name? for thou only art holy: for all nations shall come and worship before thee; for thy judgments are made manifest.

5   And after that I looked, and, behold, the temple of the tabernacle of the testimony in heaven was opened:

6   And the seven angels came out of the temple, having the seven plagues, clothed in pure and white linen, and having their breasts girded with golden girdles.

7   And one of the four beasts gave unto the seven angels seven golden vials full of the wrath of God, who liveth for ever and ever.

8   And the temple was filled with smoke from the glory of God, and from his power; and no man was able to enter into the temple, till the seven plagues of the seven angels were fulfilled.

CHAPTER 16

1   And I heard a great voice out of the temple saying to the seven angels, Go your ways, and pour out the vials of the wrath of God upon the earth.

2   And the first went, and poured out his vial upon the earth; and there fell a noisome and grievous sore upon the men which had the mark of the beast, and upon them which worshiped his image.

3   And the second angel poured out his vial upon the sea; and it became as the blood of a dead man: and every living soul died in the sea.

4   And the third angel poured out his vial upon the rivers and fountains of waters; and they became blood.

5   And I heard the angel of the waters say, Thou art righteous, O Lord, which art, and wast, and shalt be, because thou hast judged thus.

6   For they have shed the blood of saints and prophets, and thou hast given them blood to drink; for they are worthy.

7   And I heard another out of the altar say, Even so, Lord God Almighty, true and righteous are thy judgments.

8   And the fourth angel poured out his vial upon the sun; and power was given unto him to scorch men with fire.

9   And men were scorched with great heat, and blasphemed the name of God, which hath power over these plagues; and they repented not to give him glory.

10   And the fifth angel poured out his vial upon the seat of the beast; and his kingdom was full of darkness; and they gnawed their tongues for pain,

11   And blasphemed the God of heaven because of their pains and their sores, and repented not of their deeds.

12   And the sixth angel poured out his vial upon the great river Euphrates; and the water thereof was dried up, that the way of the kings of the east might be prepared.

13   And I saw three unclean spirits like frogs come out of the mouth of the dragon, and out of the mouth of the beast, and out of the mouth of the false prophet.

14   For they are the spirits of devils, working miracles, which go forth unto the kings of the earth and of the whole world, to gather them to the battle of that great day of God Almighty.

15   Behold, I come as a thief. Blessed is he that watcheth, and keepeth his garments, lest he walk naked, and they see his shame.

16   And he gathered them together into a place called in the Hebrew tongue Armageddon.

17   And the seventh angel poured out his vial into the air; and there came a great voice out of the temple of heaven, from the throne, saying, It is done.

18   And there were voices, and thunders, and lightnings; and there was a great earthquake, such as was not since men were upon the earth, so mighty an earthquake, and so great.

19   And the great city was divided into three parts, and the cities of the nations fell: and great Babylon came in remembrance before God, to give unto her the cup of the wine of the fierceness of his wrath.

20   And every island fled away, and the mountains were not found.

21   And there fell upon men a great hail out of heaven, every stone about the weight of a talent: and men blasphemed God because of the plague of the hail; for the plague thereof was exceeding great.

CHAPTER 17

1   And there came one of the seven angels which had the seven vials, and talked with me, saying unto me, Come hither; I will shew unto thee the judgment of the great whore that sitteth upon many waters:

2   With whom the kings of the earth have committed fornication, and the inhabitants of the earth have been made drunk with the wine of her fornication.

3   So he carried me away in the spirit into the wilderness: and I saw a woman sit upon a scarlet coloured beast, full of names of blasphemy, having seven heads and ten horns.

4   And the woman was arrayed in purple and scarlet colour, and decked with gold and precious stones and pearls, having a golden cup in her hand full of abominations and filthiness of her fornication:

5   And upon her forehead was a name written, MYSTERY, BABYLON THE GREAT, THE MOTHER OF HARLOTS AND ABOMINATIONS OF THE EARTH.

6   And I saw the woman drunken with the blood of the saints, and with the blood of the martyrs of Jesus: and when I saw her, I wondered with great admiration.

7   And the angel said unto me, Wherefore didst thou marvel? I will tell thee the mystery of the woman, and of the beast that carrieth her, which hath the seven heads and ten horns.

8   The beast that thou sawest was, and is not; and shall ascend out of the bottomless pit, and go into perdition: and they that dwell on the earth shall wonder, whose names were not written in the book of life from the foundation of the world, when they behold the beast that was, and is not, and yet is.

9   And here is the mind which hath wisdom. The seven heads are seven mountains, on which the woman sitteth.

10   And there are seven kings: five are fallen, and one is, and the other is not yet come; and when he cometh, he must continue a short space.

11   And the beast that was, and is not, even he is the eighth, and is of the seven, and goeth into perdition.

12   And the ten horns which thou sawest are ten kings, which have received no kingdom as yet; but receive power as kings one hour with the beast.

13   These have one mind, and shall give their power and strength unto the beast.

14   These shall make war with the Lamb, and the Lamb shall overcome them: for he is Lord of lords, and King of kings: and they that are with him are called, and chosen, and faithful.

15   And he saith unto me, the waters which thou sawest, where the whore sitteth, are peoples, and multitudes, and nations, and tongues.

16   And the ten horns which thou sawest upon the beast, these shall hate the whore, and shall make her desolate and naked, and shall eat her flesh, and burn her with fire.

17   For God hath put in their hearts to fulfil his will, and to agree, and give their kingdom unto the beast, until the words of God shall be fulfilled.

18   And the woman which thou sawest is that great city, which reigneth over the kings of the earth.

CHAPTER 18

1   And after these things I saw another angel come down from heaven, having great power; and the earth was lightened with his glory.

2   And he cried mightily with a strong voice, saying, Babylon the great is fallen, is fallen, and is become the habitation of devils, and the hold of every foul spirit, and a cage of every unclean and hateful bird.

3   For all nations have drunk of the wine of the wrath of her fornication, and the kings of the earth have committed fornication with her, and the merchants of the earth are waxed rich through the abundance of her delicacies.

4   And I heard another voice from heaven, saying, Come out of her, my people, that ye be not partakers of her sins, and that ye receive not of her plagues.

5   For her sins have reached unto heaven, and God hath remembered her iniquities.

6   Reward her even as she rewarded you, and double unto her double according to her works: in the cup which she hath filled fill to her double.

7   How much she hath glorified herself, and lived deliciously, so much torment and sorrow give her: for she saith in her heart, I sit a queen, and am no widow, and shall see no sorrow.

8   Therefore shall her plagues come in one day, death, and mourning, and famine; and she shall be utterly burned with fire: for strong is the Lord God who judgeth her.

9   And the kings of the earth, who have committed fornication and lived deliciously with her, shall bewail her, and lament for her, when they shall see the smoke of her burning,

10   Standing afar off for the fear of her torment, saying, Alas, alas, that great city Babylon, that mighty city! for in one hour is thy judgment come.

11   And the merchants of the earth shall weep and mourn over her; for no man buyeth their merchandise any more:

12   The merchandise of gold, and silver, and precious stones, and of pearls, and fine linen, and purple, and silk, and scarlet, and all thyine wood, and all manner vessels of ivory, and all manner vessels of most precious wood, and of brass, and iron, and marble,

13   And cinnamon, and odours, and ointments, and frankincense, and wine, and oil, and fine flour, and wheat, and beasts, and sheep, and horses, and chariots, and slaves, and souls of men.

14   And the fruits that thy soul lusted after are departed from thee, and all things which were dainty and goodly are departed from thee, and thou shalt find them no more at all.

15   The merchants of these things, which were made rich by her, shall stand afar off for the fear of her torment, weeping and wailing,

16   And saying, Alas, alas that great city, that was clothed in fine linen, and purple, and scarlet, and decked with gold, and precious stones, and pearls!

17   For in one hour so great riches is come to nought. And every shipmaster, and all the company in ships, and sailors, and as many as trade by sea, stood afar off,

18   And cried when they saw the smoke of her burning, saying, What city is like unto this great city!

19   And they cast dust on their heads, and cried, weeping and wailing, saying, Alas, alas that great city, wherein were made rich all that had ships in the sea by reason of her costliness! for in one hour is she made desolate.

20   Rejoice over her, thou heaven, and ye holy apostles and prophets; for God hath avenged you on her.

21   And a mighty angel took up a stone like a great millstone, and cast it into the sea, saying, Thus with violence shall that great city Babylon be thrown down, and shall be found no more at all.

22   And the voice of harpers, and musicians, and of pipers, and trumpeters, shall be heard no more at all in thee; and no craftsman, of whatsoever craft he be, shall be found any more in thee; and the sound of a millstone shall be heard no more at all in thee;

23   And the light of a candle shall shine no more at all in thee; and the voice of the bridegroom and of the bride shall be heard no more at all in thee: for thy merchants were the great men of the earth; for by thy sorceries were all nations deceived.

24   And in her was found the blood of prophets, and of saints, and of all that were slain upon the earth.

CHAPTER 19

1   And after these things I heard a great voice of much people in heaven, saying, Alleluia; Salvation, and glory, and honour, and power, unto the Lord our God:

2   For true and righteous are his judgments: for he hath judged the great whore, which did corrupt the earth with her fornication, and hath avenged the blood of his servants at her hand.

3   And again they said, Alleluia. And her smoke rose up for ever and ever.

4   And the four and twenty elders and the four beasts fell down and worshiped God that sat on the throne, saying, Amen; Alleluia.

5   And a voice came out of the throne, saying, Praise our God, all ye his servants, and ye that fear him, both small and great.

6   And I heard as it were the voice of a great multitude, and as the voice of many waters, and as the voice of mighty thunderings, saying, Alleluia: for the Lord God omnipotent reigneth.

7   Let us be glad and rejoice, and give honour to him: for the marriage of the Lamb is come, and his wife hath made herself ready.

8   And to her was granted that she should be arrayed in fine linen, clean and white: for the fine linen is the righteousness of saints.

9   And he saith unto me, Write, Blessed are they which are called unto the marriage supper of the Lamb. And he saith unto me, These are the true sayings of God.

10   And I fell at his feet to worship him. And he said unto me, See thou do it not: I am thy fellowservant, and of thy brethren that have the testimony of Jesus: worship God: for the testimony of Jesus is the spirit of prophecy.

11   And I saw heaven opened, and behold a white horse; and he that sat upon him was called Faithful and True, and in righteousness he doth judge and make war.

12   His eyes were as a flame of fire, and on his head were many crowns; and he had a name written, that no man knew, but he himself.

13   And he was clothed with a vesture dipped in blood: and his name is called The Word of God.

14   And the armies which were in heaven followed him upon white horses, clothed in fine linen, white and clean.

15   And out of his mouth goeth a sharp sword, that with it he should smite the nations: and he shall rule them with a rod of iron: and he treadeth the winepress of the fierceness and wrath of Almighty God.

16   And he hath on his vesture and on his thigh a name written, KING OF KINGS, AND LORD OF LORDS.

17   And I saw an angel standing in the sun; and he cried with a loud voice, saying to all the fowls that fly in the midst of heaven, Come and gather yourselves together unto the supper of the great God;

18   That ye may eat the flesh of kings, and the flesh of captains, and the flesh of mighty men, and the flesh of horses, and of them that sit on them, and the flesh of all men, both free and bond, both small and great.

19   And I saw the beast, and the kings of the earth, and their armies, gathered together to make war against him that sat on the horse, and against his army.

20   And the beast was taken, and with him the false prophet that wrought miracles before him, with which he deceived them that had received the mark of the beast, and them that worshiped his image. These both were cast alive into a lake of fire burning with brimstone.

21   And the remnant were slain with the sword of him that sat upon the horse, which sword proceeded out of his mouth: and all the fowls were filled with their flesh.

CHAPTER 20

1   And I saw an angel come down from heaven, having the key of the bottomless pit and a great chain in his hand.

2   And he laid hold on the dragon, that old serpent, which is the Devil, and Satan, and bound him a thousand years,

3   And cast him into the bottomless pit, and shut him up, and set a seal upon him, that he should deceive the nations no more, till the thousand years should be fulfilled: and after that he must be loosed a little season.

4   And I saw thrones, and they sat upon them, and judgment was given unto them: and I saw the souls of them that were beheaded for the witness of Jesus, and for the word of God, and which had not worshiped the beast, neither his image, neither had received his mark upon their foreheads, or in their hands; and they lived and reigned with Christ a thousand years.

5   But the rest of the dead lived not again until the thousand years were finished. This is the first resurrection.

6   Blessed and holy is he that hath part in the first resurrection: on such the second death hath no power, but they shall be priests of God and of Christ, and shall reign with him a thousand years.

7   And when the thousand years are expired, Satan shall be loosed out of his prison,

8   And shall go out to deceive the nations which are in the four quarters of the earth, Gog, and Magog, to gather them together to battle: the number of whom is as the sand of the sea.

9   And they went up on the breadth of the earth, and compassed the camp of the saints about, and the beloved city: and fire came down from God out of heaven, and devoured them.

10   And the devil that deceived them was cast into the lake of fire and brimstone, where the beast and the false prophet are, and shall be tormented day and night for ever and ever.

11   And I saw a great white throne, and him that sat on it, from whose face the earth and the heaven fled away; and there was found no place for them.

12   And I saw the dead, small and great, stand before God; and the books were opened: and another book was opened, which is the book of life: and the dead were judged out of those things which were written in the books, according to their works.

13   And the sea gave up the dead which were in it; and death and hell delivered up the dead which were in them: and they were judged every man according to their works.

14   And death and hell were cast into the lake of fire. This is the second death.

15   And whosoever was not found written in the book of life was cast into the lake of fire.

CHAPTER 21

1   And I saw a new heaven and a new earth: for the first heaven and the first earth were passed away; and there was no more sea.

2   And I John saw the holy city, new Jerusalem, coming down from God out of heaven, prepared as a bride adorned for her husband.

3   And I heard a great voice out of heaven saying, Behold, the tabernacle of God is with men, and he will dwell with them, and they shall be his people, and God himself shall be with them, and be their God.

4   And God shall wipe away all tears from their eyes; and there shall be no more death, neither sorrow, nor crying, neither shall there be any more pain: for the former things are passed away.

5   And he that sat upon the throne said, Behold, I make all things new. And he said unto me, Write: for these words are true and faithful.

6   And he said unto me, It is done. I am Alpha and Omega, the beginning and the end. I will give unto him that is athirst of the fountain of the water of life freely.

7   He that overcometh shall inherit all things; and I will be his God, and he shall be my son.

8   But the fearful, and unbelieving, and the abominable, and murderers, and whoremongers, and sorcerers, and idolaters, and all liars, shall have their part in the lake which burneth with fire and brimstone: which is the second death.

9   And there came unto me one of the seven angels which had the seven vials full of the seven last plagues, and talked with me, saying, Come hither, I will shew thee the bride, the Lamb's wife.

10   And he carried me away in the spirit to a great and high mountain, and shewed me that great city, the holy Jerusalem, descending out of heaven from God,

11   Having the glory of God: and her light was like unto a stone most precious, even like a jasper stone, clear as crystal;

12   And had a wall great and high, and had twelve gates, and at the gates twelve angels, and names written thereon, which are the names of the twelve tribes of the children of Israel:

13   On the east three gates; on the north three gates; on the south three gates; and on the west three gates.

14   And the wall of the city had twelve foundations, and in them the names of the twelve apostles of the Lamb.

15   And he that talked with me had a golden reed to measure the city, and the gates thereof, and the wall thereof.

16   And the city lieth foursquare, and the length is as large as the breadth: and he measured the city with the reed, twelve thousand furlongs. The length and the breadth and the height of it are equal.

17   And he measured the wall thereof, an hundred and forty and four cubits, according to the measure of a man, that is, of the angel.

18   And the building of the wall of it was of jasper: and the city was pure gold, like unto clear glass.

19   And the foundations of the wall of the city were garnished with all manner of precious stones. The first foundation was jasper; the second, sapphire; the third, a chalcedony; the fourth, an emerald;

20   The fifth, sardonyx; the sixth, sardius; the seventh, chrysolyte; the eighth, beryl; the ninth, a topaz; the tenth, a chrysoprasus; the eleventh, a jacinth; the twelfth, an amethyst.

21   And the twelve gates were twelve pearls: every several gate was of one pearl: and the street of the city was pure gold, as it were transparent glass.

22   And I saw no temple therein: for the Lord God Almighty and the Lamb are the temple of it.

23   And the city had no need of the sun, neither of the moon, to shine in it: for the glory of God did lighten it, and the Lamb is the light thereof.

24   And the nations of them which are saved shall walk in the light of it: and the kings of the earth do bring their glory and honour into it.

25   And the gates of it shall not be shut at all by day: for there shall be no night there.

26 And they shall bring the glory and honour of the nations into it.

27   And there shall in no wise enter into it any thing that defileth, neither whatsoever worketh abomination, or maketh a lie: but they which are written in the Lamb's book of life.

CHAPTER 22

1   And he shewed me a pure river of water of life, clear as crystal, proceeding out of the throne of God and of the Lamb.

2   In the midst of the street of it, and on either side of the river, was there the tree of life, which bare twelve manner of fruits, and yielded her fruit every month: and the leaves of the tree were for the healing of the nations.

3   And there shall be no more curse: but the throne of God and of the Lamb shall be in it; and his servants shall serve him:

4   And they shall see his face; and his name shall be in their foreheads.

5   And there shall be no night there; and they need no candle, neither light of the sun; for the Lord God giveth them light: and they shall reign for ever and ever.

6   And he said unto me, These sayings are faithful and true: and the Lord God of the holy prophets sent his angel to shew unto his servants the things which must shortly be done.

7   Behold, I come quickly: blessed is he that keepeth the sayings of the prophecy of this book.

8   And I John saw these things, and heard them. And when I had heard and seen, I fell down to worship before the feet of the angel which shewed me these things.

9   Then saith he unto me, See thou do it not: for I am thy fellowservant, and of thy brethren the prophets, and of them which keep the sayings of this book: worship God.

10   And he saith unto me, Seal not the sayings of the prophecy of this book: for the time is at hand.

11   He that is unjust, let him be unjust still: and he which is filthy, let him be filthy still: and he that is righteous, let him be righteous still: and he that is holy, let him be holy still.

12   And, behold, I come quickly; and my reward is with me, to give every man according as his work shall be.

13   I am Alpha and Omega, the beginning and the end, the first and the last.

14   Blessed are they that do his commandments, that they may have right to the tree of life, and may enter in through the gates into the city.

15   For without are dogs, and sorcerers, and whoremongers, and mur- derers, and idolaters, and whosoever loveth and maketh a lie.

16   I Jesus have sent mine angel to testify unto you these things in the churches. I am the root and the offspring of David, and the bright and morning star.

17   And the Spirit and the bride say, Come. And let him that heareth say, Come. And let him that is athirst come. And whosoever will, let him take the water of life freely.

18   For I testify unto every man that heareth the words of the prophecy of this book, If any man shall add unto these things, God shall add unto him the plagues that are written in this book:

19   And if any man shall take away from the words of the book of this prophecy, God shall take away his part out of the book of life, and out of the holy city, and from the things which are written in this book.

20   He which testifieth these things saith, Surely I come quickly. Amen. Even so, come, Lord Jesus.

21   The grace of our Lord Jesus Christ be with you all. Amen.

BIBLIOGRAPHY

Achtemeier, Paul J. (ed.). *Harper's Bible Dictionary*. San Francisco: Harper-Collins, 1985.

Asimov, Isaac. *Asimov's Guide to the Bible*. New York: Avenel Books, 1981.

Borges, Jorge Luis. *Other Inquisitions: 1937–1952*. Austin, TX: University of Texas Press, 1965.

———. *A Personal Anthology*. New York: Castle Books (in association with Grove Press), 1967.

Budge, E. A. Wallis. *The Egyptian Book of the Dead* (1895). New York: Dover Reprint, 1967.

———. *Egyptian Magic*. (1901). New York: Dover Reprint, 1971.

———. *The Gods of the Egyptians*. (1904). New York: Dover Reprint, 1969.

Comay, Joan & Brownrigg, Ronald. *Who's Who in the Bible*. New York: Bonanza Books, 1980.

Eliade, Mircea. *The Sacred and the Profane*. New York & London: Harvest, 1959.

Edinger, Edward F. *The Bible and the Psyche*. Toronto: Inner City Books, 1986.

———. *The Creation of Consciousness*. Toronto: Inner City Books, 1984.

Faulkner, William. *Absalom, Absalom*. New York: Random House, 1951.

———. *The Sound and the Fury*. New York: Random House, 1967.

Ferguson, Marilyn. "Karl Pribram's Changing Reality." In *Brain/Mind Bulletin*. Reprinted in Ken Wilber (ed.). *The Holographic Paradigm*. Boston: Shambhala, 1982.

Fox, Matthew (ed.). *Illuminations of Hildegard of Bingen*. Santa Fe, NM: Bear & Co., 1985.

———. *Hildegard of Bingen's Book of Divine Works*. Santa Fe, NM: Bear & Co., 1987.

von Franz, Marie-Louise. *Number and Time*. Evanston, IL: Northwestern University Press, 1974.

———. *C. G. Jung: His Myth in Our Time*. New York: G. P. Putnam's Sons, 1975.

Gleick, James. *Chaos: Making a New Science*. New York: Viking Press, 1987.

Green, Roger Lancelyn. *Tales of Ancient Egypt*. New York: Penguin, 1967.

Guirand, Felix. *New Larousse Encyclopedia of Mythology*. London: Hamlyn Publishing Group, 1959.

Hall, Edward T. *The Hidden Dimension*. Garden City: Anchor Books, 1966.

Hildegard of Bingen. *Hildegard of Bingen Scivias*. Bruce Hozeski, trans. Santa Fe: Bear & Co., 1985.

Hughes, Patrick & Brecht, George. *Vicious Circles and Infinity: an Anthology of Paradoxes*. New York: Penguin, 1978.

Jung, C. G. *Collected Works*. Princeton: Bollingen Series, Princeton University Press.

Kastner, Joseph (ed. and trans.). *Wings of the Falcon: Life and Thought of Ancient Egypt*. New York: Holt, Rinehart & Winston, 1968.

Levi, Primo. *The Periodic Table*. New York: Schocken Books, 1984.

Lorenz, Konrad. *King Solomon's Ring*. New York: Crowell, 1952.

Loye, David. *The Sphinx and the Rainbow*. New York: Bantam Books, 1983.

McLuhan, Marshall. *The Gutenberg Galaxy*. Toronto: University of Toronto Press, 1962.

McLuhan, Marshall & Fiore, Quentin. *The Medium is the Massage*. New York: Bantam Books, 1967.

McKenzie, John L., S. J. *Dictionary of the Bible*. New York: Macmillan, 1965.

"The Perfect Pitch" (newsletter), July 22, 1985.

Poincare, Henri, 1903. *Science and Method*, Mineola, NY: Dover Publications, reprint 1952.

Pribram, Karl. "The Brain." In Alberto Villoldo and Ken Dychtwald (eds.). *Millennium: Glimpses into the 21st Century*. Los Angeles: J. P. Tarcher, 1981.

Reese, W. L. *Dictionary of Philosophy and Religion*. Atlantic Highlands, NJ: Humanities Press, 1980.

Robertson, Robin. *C. G. Jung and the Archetypes of the Collective Unconscious*. New York: Peter Lang Publishing, 1987. Revised edition to publish in 1995 as *Beginner's Guide to Archetypes*.

Sheldrake, Rupert. "Mind, Memory and Archetype." In *Psychological Perspectives*, Los Angeles: C. G. Jung Institute, Spring 1987.

Toms, Michael. "An Interview With John Kimmey." San Francisco: New Dimensions Radio, Tape #1741, 1987.

Uhlein, Gabriele (ed. & trans.). *Meditations with Hildegard of Bingen*. Santa Fe, NM: Bear & Co., 1983.

Waters, Frank. *Book of the Hopi*. New York: Penguin, 1977.

———. *Pumpkin Seed Point*. Athens, OH: Sage Books, 1969.

Watson, Peter. *Twins: An Uncanny Relationship*. New York: Viking Press, 1982.

Wilhelm Richard, trans. *The I Ching*, 3rd ed. Princeton: Princeton University Press, Bollingen Series XIX, 1977.

INDEX

Robin Robertson has a B. S. in Mathematics and a B. A. in English Literature from the University of Maryland. He went on to earn a M. A. in Counseling Psychology and a Ph. D. in Clinical Psychology. From 1986 to 1990, he served as staff editor and wrote book reviews for *Psychological Perspectives,* a Jungian journal. He is the author of *Beginner's Guide to Jungian Psychology* (also Published by Nicolas-Hays) and is currently at work on *Beginner'sGuide to the Archetypes*.